EZRA
THROUGH
ESTHER

WESLEY BIBLE STUDIES

wphstore.com

Copyright © 2015 by Wesleyan Publishing House
Published by Wesleyan Publishing House
Indianapolis, Indiana 46250
Printed in the United States of America
ISBN: 978-0-89827-842-2
ISBN (e-book): 978-0-89827-843-9

All Scripture quotations, unless otherwise indicated, are taken from the Holy Bible, New International Version®, NIV®. Copyright ©1973, 1978, 1984 by Biblica, Inc. Used by permission of Zondervan. All rights reserved worldwide. www.zondervan.com. The "NIV" and "New International Version" are trademarks registered in the United States Patent and Trademark Office by Biblica, Inc.

Cover image © iStockphoto LP 2013. All rights reserved. Engraving by Gustave Dore (1832–1883). Esther accuses Haman of treachery

All rights reserved. No part of this publication may be reproduced, stored in a retrieval system, or transmitted in any form or by any means—electronic, mechanical, photocopy, recording, or any other—except for brief quotations in printed reviews, without the prior written permission of the publisher.

CONTENTS

Introduction	5
1. God Leaves Nothing to Chance Ezra 1:1–11; 2:64–70	7
2. The Joy of New Beginnings Ezra 3:1–6; 3:10—4:5	16
3. God's Plan Is Not Detoured Ezra 6:1–3, 13–22	25
4. Going Where God Is Leading Ezra 7:6–10, 27–28; 8:21–23, 31–32, 35–36	34
5. Handling God-Given Burdens Nehemiah 1:1–11; 2:4–5, 11–12, 17–18	42
6. Victory in Adversity Nehemiah 4:1–15, 19–20	51
7. Fightings Within Nehemiah 5:1–13	59
8. The Power of the Word Nehemiah 8:1–10, 18; 9:1–3	68
9. The Foolish King and the Wise Virgin Esther 1:2–4, 10–12; 2:1–2, 5–7, 15, 17–18	76
10. The Varied Faces of Evil Esther 2:19–23; 3:1–6, 8–11	85
11. Godly Character Meets Challenges with Godliness Esther 4:1, 4; 4:12—5:9	93
12. God Honors Righteousness and Faithfulness Esther 6:1–10; 7:1–10; 10:3	101
Words from Wesley Works Cited	110

INTRODUCTION

God Is in Control

There was no way US Airways Flight 1549 could land at an airport on January 15, 2009. A flock of birds had snuffed out the engines. However, Captain Chesley Sullenberger was in control and safely landed his plane in the Hudson River. The crew and all 155 passengers survived. The incident became known as the "Miracle on the Hudson," and Captain "Sully" was hailed as a hero. But far above the Hudson, God was in control of the airline mishap.

We cannot read the books of Ezra, Nehemiah, and Esther without recognizing that God rules over history. He allowed the Babylonians to uproot His people from their homeland and transplant them to Babylon because they had bowed to false gods and violated the Sabbath. But He protected them in Babylon, and later when Babylon was conquered by Persia. Eventually, He intervened in history to restore them to their homeland.

THE RETURN FROM CAPTIVITY

God had prophesied through the prophet Isaiah that King Cyrus of Persia would initiate the Jews' return (Isa. 45:13). The prophecy was fulfilled in the first year of Cyrus's reign (Ezra 1:1). Perhaps the king wanted to show goodwill to the conquered people groups in his empire and by doing so gain the favor of their gods. He acknowledged that the Jews' God had appointed him to build Him a temple at Jerusalem. Therefore, Cyrus allowed the Jews to leave Persia and begin the construction project in Jerusalem.

THE REBUILDING OF THE TEMPLE

The returnees succeeded in building the altar and the foundation, but then they encountered opposition. Nevertheless, God overruled the opposition and moved the heart of King Darius to issue a decree calling for widespread support of the project. Because God was in control, the temple project was completed.

THE RECONSTRUCTION OF JERUSALEM'S WALLS

We learn from the book of Nehemiah that God answers prayer. In answer to Nehemiah's prayer, He moved the heart of King Artaxerxes to grant Nehemiah permission to return to Jerusalem to reconstruct its walls. Because He was in control, He enabled the builders to overcome ridicule, military opposition, and discouragement, and finish their work.

A YOUNG WOMAN'S LIFE

Although God's name does not appear in the book of Esther, His providential control beams from its pages. We learn how He brought Esther to the kingdom of Persia for the purpose of saving the Jews from annihilation. We cannot read her story without seeing that it is His story. He orchestrated the events that unfold in the book of Esther so that the villain Haman went to the gallows prepared for Esther's devout cousin, Mordecai, and the people marked for annihilation survived.

OUR LIVES

By studying the books of Ezra, Nehemiah, and Esther, we gain strong faith and confidence in God. We see that He cares for His people and is in control of their lives. Nothing surprises Him, topples Him from His throne, or takes control from Him.

GOD LEAVES NOTHING TO CHANCE

Ezra 1:1–11; 2:64–70

God moves the hearts of people to fulfill His plan.

It is easy to despair about alarming world events. So many world leaders seem determined to obliterate our way of life that we may think our religious freedom is short-lived. However, the story of Cyrus's decree encourages us to lift our eyes and hearts toward God.

By observing God at work in Cyrus's heart, you will respond to the daily news not with despair but with confidence in God's ability to transform desperate situations into opportunities to display His power.

COMMENTARY

God's patience had run out. He had always proven himself faithful to His chosen people, Israel. But from the time He delivered them from Egypt, they continually rebelled against Him and worshiped other gods. Time and again, they were warned by prophets to return to the Lord, but to no avail. Finally, God pronounced judgment. In 722–721 B.C., the kingdom of Israel (the ten northern tribes) was crushed by the Assyrian Empire. God's people were taken into captivity, and the area was repopulated with captives from other lands. The kingdom of Judah (the tribes of Judah and Benjamin) should have realized that the same fate awaited them, but they didn't. They continued in their apostasy. It was just a matter of time before God brought judgment on them as well.

Ezra 1:1–11; 2:64–70

In 612 B.C., Nineveh, the capital of Assyria, fell to the Babylonians and soon after, the Assyrian empire crumbled. In 605, the Egyptians were crushed at Carchemish by Nebuchadnezzar, and Babylon became the dominant world power. That same year, the Babylonians besieged Jerusalem and took a large number of captives into exile, including the prophet Daniel. Later, in 597, all the skilled craftsmen, artisans, and officials (including Jehoiachin, king of Judah, and probably the prophet Ezekiel) were also carried off to exile in Babylon. The final blow came in 586. After an eighteen-month siege, Jerusalem fell to the Babylonians, who quickly burned every important building, including the temple of the Lord. The walls surrounding the city were broken down, and all but the poorest people were taken into exile.

None of these events happened by accident; they were the direct result of Israel's and Judah's sin against the Lord. God had His hand in the political events that transpired to bring judgment on His own people: "It was because of the LORD's anger that all this happened to Jerusalem and Judah, and in the end he thrust them from his presence" (2 Kings 24:20).

So, God's people found themselves in a foreign country. The temple, which represented God's presence, had been utterly destroyed. What now? Was God completely finished with them? Was there room for forgiveness and restoration? Or had God abandoned them for good?

The exiles might have thought God was through with them. But He was still working behind the scenes to bring about His will. Through the prophet Jeremiah, God had promised, even before the fall of Jerusalem, that they would return (see Jer. 29:10; 25:11–12). The prophet Isaiah, writing 150 years earlier, foretold the name of the king who would allow the exiles to return (see Isa. 44:28; 45:1, 13). God had not forgotten about His people.

God Leaves Nothing to Chance

In 539 B.C., the Babylonian Empire gave way to the Medo-Persian Empire. Daniel foretold it after the "writing on the wall" (Dan. 5). "That very night Belshazzar, king of the Babylonians, was slain, and Darius the Mede took over the kingdom, at the age of sixty-two" (Dan. 5:30–31). Darius was probably a throne name for Cyrus and shouldn't be confused with the later Persian king by that name. Cyrus, king of Persia, took Babylon without a fight. The people welcomed him as a liberator and gave him the title "King of Babylon," which was considered the highest honor in the civilized world at that time.

The book of Ezra begins in 538 B.C., in the first full year of the reign of Cyrus. Ezra's account begins with Cyrus's proclamation allowing the exiles to return to their homeland and to rebuild the temple in Jerusalem (also found in 2 Chron. 36:22–23). Unlike the Babylonian kings who carried off the "gods" of captive nations, Cyrus was moved to generosity and kindness toward the exiles. According to the Cyrus Cylinder, which dates to 538 B.C., Cyrus's motive may have been to invoke the favor of the gods of the captive nations. He wrote, "May all the gods whom I have resettled in their sacred cities daily ask Bel and Nebo for a long life for me." But Ezra says, whatever Cyrus's motive, it was the Lord who moved the heart of Cyrus (1:1). According to the Jewish historian Josephus, Cyrus was shown the prophecy of Isaiah 44:28 and desired to fulfill it (*The Antiquities of Josephus*, 11.1.1). Maybe it was Daniel himself who pointed out the prophecy to Cyrus (see Dan. 9:1–3), and perhaps it was even Daniel's exemplary witness that prompted Cyrus's generosity toward the Jews (see Dan. 6:3). In any case, Ezra makes plain that God was involved in the proclamation that was made. He had foretold and willed it. The Persian king was an instrument in His hands.

The Proclamation of Cyrus (Ezra 1:1–4)

Not only did Cyrus issue an oral **proclamation** (v. 1, recorded in Hebrew here in 1:2–4), but he also **put it in writing** (recorded in Aramaic, the international language of the Persian Empire, in 6:3–5). Although probably not a true believer in the God of Israel, Cyrus attributed his military success to **the LORD, the God of heaven** (v. 2), and he also understood (probably from Isaiah's prophecy) that God **has appointed me to build a temple for him at Jerusalem in Judah**. The purpose of the proclamation was twofold: (1) to encourage the Jews in exile to return to Jerusalem to rebuild the temple (see v. 3); and (2) to urge their non-Israelite neighbors, or Jews not wishing to resettle in Judah (**the people of any place where survivors may now be living**, v. 4), to provide the returning Jews with **silver and gold, with goods and livestock, and with freewill offerings for the temple** (v. 4; see also v. 6).

Notice the similarity between this event and the Israelites' exodus from Egypt nine hundred years earlier: "The Israelites did as Moses instructed and asked the Egyptians for articles of silver and gold and for clothing. The LORD had made the Egyptians favorably disposed toward the people, and they gave them what they asked for; so they plundered the Egyptians" (Ex. 12:35–36). No wonder the return from captivity in Babylon was later referred to as the "Second Exodus." This act of favor reminded them of God's deliverance and graciousness toward them in the past, and it rekindled hope that God was still looking out for them.

The Preparation of Judah (Ezra 1:5–11; 2:64–70)

Not only had God moved the heart of Cyrus (1:1), but He also moved the hearts of His people: **everyone whose heart God had moved ... prepared to go up and build the house of the LORD in Jerusalem** (1:5). However, not all the exiles desired to resettle in Judah. Many of the captives had fared well in Babylon and Persia. They had acquired land and were comfortable. Since the exile had begun almost seventy years earlier, many Jews currently living in Persia had been born there. Ezra himself had not yet been born at the time of this first return to Judah. Many of those born in captivity had little attachment to the homeland and no desire to return. But God stirred the hearts of some. Some remembered the Promised Land. Others had learned about it from faithful parents who passed down traditions and taught them the Scriptures as commanded in Deuteronomy 6:4–9. And they yearned to return. It was a yearning placed in their hearts by God, a yearning to be in His presence in His land, a yearning to be restored to favor with God.

WORDS FROM WESLEY

Ezra 1:5

Then rose up—These being a new generation, went out like their father Abraham, from this land of the Chaldees, not knowing whither they went. (ENOT)

The tribes of **Judah and Benjamin** (Ezra 1:5) are mentioned specifically, since most of the exiles were from these two tribes (which comprised the southern kingdom of Judah). The **Levites**, of course, would also have been represented, since they were allotted towns throughout Israel and Judah and had been involved in the care of the temple at Jerusalem at the time of the Babylonian conquest. But all the tribes were likely represented in part, so that those who returned could rightfully be called the remnant of all Israel. Second Chronicles makes frequent mention of the migration of peoples from the tribes in the north to the southern kingdom (11:14; 15:9; 30:6–11, 18; 31:6; 34:9). This could also account for the considerable difference between the number of returnees listed in Ezra 2:3–61 and the total of **42,360** recorded in 2:64.

In preparation for their return to Jerusalem and their rebuilding of the temple, **Cyrus brought out the articles belonging to the temple of the L**ORD**, which Nebuchadnezzar had carried away from Jerusalem and had placed in the temple of his god** (1:7). Nebuchadnezzar had done what was customary—to take from captives the symbols of their gods. Military conquest was largely seen as the triumph of one god over another, but since the Israelites had no physical representation of their god, the articles of the temple were taken as a substitute. While only 2,499 articles are listed, the author tells us **in all, there were 5,400 articles of gold and of silver** (1:11). This was quite a generous concession on Cyrus's part.

WORDS FROM WESLEY
Ezra 1:6

Strengthened their hands—God can, when He pleases, incline the hearts of strangers to be kind to His people; yea, make those strengthen their hands, who formerly weakened them. (ENOT)

Verse 11 of chapter 1 also mentions a man named **Sheshbazzar**. Some scholars believe that since both Sheshbazzar and Zerubbabel are credited with laying the foundation of the temple (3:2–8; 5:16) and both were considered governors (5:14; Hag. 1:1; 2:2), Sheshbazzar is simply a Persian name for Zerubbabel (whose name means "begotten in Babel"). Others believe he is to be identified with Shenazzar in 1 Chronicles 3:17, making him Zerubbabel's uncle. Still others hold he was a Persian official sent to oversee the return and rebuilding and to protect the king's interests.

Altogether, 49,897 men, women, and children returned with Zerubbabel (and/or Sheshbazzar) to repopulate the land of Judah. That includes **7,337 menservants and maidservants** (2:65) who probably were not of Jewish ancestry and **200 men and women singers** (probably secular, since temple singers are specifically listed in 2:41). It speaks well of the Jews and their treatment of servants that such a large number would choose to return with them to Judah. The trek from Babylon/Persia (modern-day Iraq and Iran) was nine hundred miles and would take four months. This is probably why no cattle, sheep, and goats were taken along, only **camels** and **donkeys** (2:67), which were suited for such a long trip.

Many years before, when God had led His people in the exodus from Egypt, they had counted 603,550 men of military age (Ex. 38:26). There would have been 1.5 million to 3 million people total in Israel at that time. God had truly blessed Abraham's descendents. But in 722 B.C. the northern kingdom had been decimated. It is estimated that the sixth-century population of Judah was only 220,000 to 300,000. Many were killed by the Babylonians. Some of the poorest had remained in Judah, but a considerable number had gone into exile. How sad that now the people of Israel (those who chose to return to the Lord and to the Promised Land) numbered fewer than 50,000. It is a tragic commentary on the consequences of sin and rebellion against God.

WORDS FROM WESLEY
Ezra 2:68

The house—That is, to the ruins of the house; or to the place were it stood. (ENOT)

When they arrived at the house of the LORD (that is, the place where the temple had stood), they **gave freewill offerings toward the rebuilding of the house of God on its site** (2:68). **According to their ability** (2:69) they gave the equivalent of eleven hundred pounds of gold and three tons of silver. A drachma (or possibly the Persian "daric") was valued at the price of an ox or a month's salary for a soldier. One mina was worth five years' wages. This offering was a fortune! God had blessed His people greatly, even in captivity.

Verse 70 ends with the people settling **in their towns**, now fully prepared to do the work God had called them to do.

WORDS FROM WESLEY
Ezra 2:70

And all Israel in their cities—And they dwelt in peace, in perfect harmony, a blessed presage of their settlement, as their discord in the latter times of that state, was of their ruin. (ENOT)

These first two chapters in Ezra should be a reminder to us in dark times that God is still moving in the hearts of His people and the rulers of this world. God has not forgotten or abandoned us. He is still in control over the events of history. And He is still working out His plan and purposes.

DISCUSSION

Because of their unfaithfulness, God's people had become captives in Babylonia. Seventy years later, as God promised, they would start returning home. Amazingly, God used a pagan king to start the process.

1. Why do you think Cyrus made a proclamation allowing the Jews to return home?
2. Why do you think Cyrus felt personally accountable to God for the building of the temple at Jerusalem?
3. How did Cyrus provide practical support for the building of the temple?
4. How does it encourage you to know that God can move a king's heart (Prov. 21:1) to accomplish His will?
5. Read Ezra 1:5. Why do you agree or disagree that a congregation should not undertake a building project unless God moves the hearts of His people to do so?
6. What did Cyrus personally donate to the temple project? Why do you think he was so generous?
7. Read verses 8–11. Why do you agree or disagree that a church should carefully account for every donation?
8. Ezra 2:68–69 reports that the returnees gave freewill offerings according to their ability. Why would you agree or disagree that Christians today should practice this manner of giving?

PRAYER

Holy Father, thank You that while You are righteous and discipline Your children, You remain merciful. Show us where our hearts are not completely Yours. And help us to see that You never give up on us.

2

THE JOY OF NEW BEGINNINGS

Ezra 3:1–6; 3:10—4:5

Joy comes when we take steps to restore the place of true worship and our relationship with God.

What pleases God more—worship or service? Is He more concerned with what we do or with who we are? When the Jews returned to Jerusalem from Babylon, they engaged in worship before they began to build the temple.

This study will inspire you to be a holy servant of God—wholly devoted to Him.

COMMENTARY

The events studied in the previous study took place after Cyrus had conquered Babylon and made it part of the Persian Empire. He built a reputation as a liberator by giving exiles the choice of returning to their homelands. Some forty thousand Jews responded. The heads of the families and their descendants who accepted Cyrus's offer to return to Judah are listed in Ezra 2.

It is interesting that of the religious ministers who returned, there were twelve times more priests than Levites. Normally, there would be far more of the latter than the former. Why might so many of the Levites decide not to return?

The nearly one-thousand-mile trek would be difficult. These Levitical servants may have felt less honor in their tasks and, therefore, did not make the sacrifices necessary for the long trip. Maybe they felt the community would do just as well without them.

Some in our churches today who are not in positions of leadership feel unnecessary and unneeded. Church leadership needs to make every effort to involve them. Likewise, the people themselves need to realize that God does not reward in proportion to rank; He rewards according to our faithfulness to the position we are given, whether high or low.

The Altar Rebuilt (Ezra 3:1-3)

By **the seventh month** (v. 1), presumably after the exiles had returned from Babylon and after they had built their houses and organized their community, their first consideration was not the temple building itself, but the sacrificial altar. This month was the most sacred of the Jewish calendar because it included some of the most solemn occasions of the year.

For fifty years, since the destruction of the first temple, the Jews had been unable to sacrifice animals, even though the law called for it. Since they did not have a temple building, they could not have a sacrificial altar to make atonement for their sins. Yet their theology still called for the blood of innocent animals to atone for the sins of the guilty sinner.

Biblical law stated that a temple was to be built only in Jerusalem. We know that synagogues sprang up during the exile as a substitute for the temple, and it appears prayer was deemed a temporary substitute for the slaying of animals. Now that they were living again in Jerusalem, there was no longer a reason to not have biblically prescribed worship. They could have a temple again!

Note that the people had their priorities in order. There was an ache in their hearts that they felt more deeply than the need for a temple. They gave first attention to the altar so they could reestablish the God-ordained method of worship.

There seems to have been no call for a national assembly. **The people** just **assembled . . . in Jerusalem** (v. 1). Since the seventh month was the time for the Day of Atonement commemoration when all sins that might have been overlooked could find atonement, the people responded. The gathering **as one man** suggests the commonality of their heartfelt need.

It was **Jeshua** (v. 2, Joshua), the leader, and other **priests**, along with **Zerubbabel**, the governor, and his **associates** who set about reconstructing the **altar** so that **burnt offerings** could be offered. The Mosaic law had commanded that there be a continual, day-and-night burnt offering on the altar (Num. 28:3–6). A lamb was to be offered every **morning** and every **evening** (Ezra 3:3) to remind Israel of her devotion to God.

The people were motivated by their need for atonement, but there was also a **fear of the peoples around them** (v. 3). The returned exiles had good cause to be afraid. The neighbors were apparently not happy with the Jews coming back to occupy the land they considered their own; they certainly did not want them to build a temple.

WORDS FROM WESLEY
Ezra 3:3

For fear—So they made the more haste, lest they should be hindered. Apprehension of dangers should quicken us in our duty. Have we many enemies? We have the more need to have God for our friend and to keep up our correspondence with Him. (ENOT)

While fear is not the best reason for coming to God, it certainly is often a motivation that causes people to turn to the Lord. But every Christian should at some point serve God not out of fear but out of love. In the same way that love must be the all-encompassing bond with a couple's commitment to each other, love should be the motivation for a Christian's commitment to the Lord.

Sacrifices Resumed (Ezra 3:4–6)

The next holy day after the Day of Atonement, which was on the tenth of the month, was the **Feast of Tabernacles** (v. 4) on the fifteenth. This feast was intended to mark the end of the harvest season and remind the people of their wilderness sojourn when they had to live in tents (Lev. 23:33–43). It was a joyous celebration that lasted seven days. During this time, the people lived in booths made of tree branches from which fruit was hung. Solomon chose to dedicate the first temple on this festival. How fitting a time to prepare to build the second one.

After that . . . the New Moon (Ezra 3:5) offerings were kept. Since the Jews followed the lunar calendar, each month began with the new moon. On those twelve (or in some years, thirteen) days of the year, Moses had commanded that the people "present to the LORD a burnt offering of two young bulls, one ram and seven male lambs a year old, all without defect" (Num. 28:11–12).

WORDS FROM WESLEY
Ezra 3:5

Offering—The morning and evening sacrifice. The law required much; but they offered more; for tho' they had little wealth, they had much zeal. Happy they that bring with them out of the furnace of affliction, such a holy heat as this! (ENOT)

The people also kept **all the appointed sacred feasts** (Ezra 3:5; see Lev. 23:2ff.). These were considered compulsory and were done on a group basis. But the people also made their observance personal, for they willingly offered **freewill offerings to the LORD**. The genuineness of our relationship to the Lord can be ascertained by our openness and willingness to give. It should be considered an act of worship just as important as prayer. Paul certainly had this in mind when he admonished, "On the first day of every week, each one of you should set aside a sum of money in keeping with his income" (1 Cor. 16:2).

In verses 3–6, the **burnt offering** is mentioned four times. This offering differed from the sin and iniquity offerings in that it emphasized the self-dedication of the worshiper to God. Effective corporate worship must begin with genuine individual commitment on the part of each worshiper.

Foundation Relayed (Ezra 3:10–13)

With the altar rebuilt, the sacrifices again in place, the sacred feasts being observed, and the offerings reinstituted, the people were now ready to lay the foundation of the temple. After another seven months (3:8), this work began.

WORDS FROM WESLEY

Ezra 3:11

Rock of eternity,
Thy church is built on Thee,
Thou the Foundation art,
Laid in the faithful heart,
And fill'd with glorious joy unknown,
We shout to see Thy house begun.
The sure Foundation laid
Makes all Thy people glad,
Who wait, with joy renew'd,
To see the house of God
In finish'd holiness arise,
By just degrees to reach the skies. (PW, vol. 9, 218)

On joyous occasions, **priests in their vestments and with trumpets, and the Levites ... with cymbals** (v. 10) made a joyful noise to the Lord (see Num. 10:8). It is thought the trumpet was a long, straight, slender metal tube whose tones would change according to the position of the lips. One is pictured on the inside of the Arch of Titus in Rome, an arch made in celebration of the fall of Jerusalem in A.D. 70 to the Romans.

Solomon's temple was destroyed by Nebuchadnezzar in 586 B.C. The occasion of this lesson is 536 B.C., fifty years later. Many, if not most, people **shouted for joy** (Ezra 3:12) when the work was completed. But all those, perhaps age sixty and over, whose memories recalled the magnificence of that first temple, could not rejoice. This small beginning brought tears to their eyes. They may also have **wept** in sorrow over the memories of the tragic events that had happened since the destruction of that most beautiful edifice.

Adversaries Rejected (Ezra 4:1–5)

Perhaps it was the noise of the shouting, but the news of the activity of the Jews quickly came to the attention of **the enemies of Judah and Benjamin** (v. 1). Though there were other peoples in the vicinity who became agitated at what was happening in Jerusalem, it was mainly the Samaritans.

When the Assyrians had conquered Israel, with the fall of its capital city of Samaria in 722 B.C., King Sargon decided to prevent further uprisings by pressing some fighting men into his chariot division and deporting many others.

Second Kings 17 tells us the Assyrians "brought people from Babylon, Cuthah, Avva, Hamath and Sepharvaim and settled them in the towns of Samaria to replace the Israelites" (v. 24). These foreigners came with their own gods and set them in the shrines and high places the people of Samaria had made (v. 30). They even engaged in the onerous practice of sacrificing children to these gods (v. 31).

The people did not substitute another religion as much as they diluted the genuine worship of the Lord with heathen practices. The Chronicler concluded, "They worshiped the LORD, but they also served their own gods in accordance with the customs of the nations from which they had been brought" (2 Kings 17:33). Then he showed the progression of the false religion and the decline of the genuine. "To this day they persist in their former practices. They neither worship the LORD nor adhere to the decrees and ordinances" (v. 34).

This mixed-race people continued to live in the land of Israel. Since they had lived in the town of Samaria, they became known as Samaritans. Through the time of the Jewish exile, they had spread southward toward Jerusalem.

It is impossible to know with certainty the motive of these Samaritans. Many commentators are of the opinion they only requested, **Let us help you build** (Ezra 4:2), to sabotage the effort from within, to make the edifice weak, or in some other way to hinder the work. They would have been concerned about their own security and power, and they would have been aware of the history of the Jews' opposition to anything that put a lid on their independence.

Some scholars have suggested that the Samaritans were sincere in their desire to unite with the Jews in common worship. If this is so, **Zerubbabel, Jeshua and the rest of the heads of the families** (v. 3) realized that to accept the offer would certainly weaken their faith by giving greater recognition to other gods and by not accepting all the Scripture.

In either case, the offer was rejected out of hand: **You have no part with us in building a temple to our God** (v. 3). The phrase **our God** may show that the Jews felt that the God the Samaritans had been sacrificing to **since the days of Esarhaddon** (v. 2) was a different god than the one they served.

> ## WORDS FROM WESLEY
> ### Ezra 4:3
>
> *With us*—As being of another nation and religion, and therefore not concerned in Cyrus's grant, which was confined to the Israelites. Take heed, whom you go partners with, and on whose hand you lean. While we trust God with an absolute confidence, we must trust men with a prudent caution. (ENOT)

Opposition to further work on the temple was immediate. The Hebrew literally says they "weakened the hands of the people of Judah" (v. 4). The phrase means "a continual process of discouragement." Then we are told how long the interference lasted—**during the entire reign of Cyrus . . . and down to the reign of Darius** (v. 5). Cyrus's reign ended in 529 B.C. He was succeeded by Cambyses, who reigned from 529 to 522 B.C. A usurper followed for only seven months, who was then deposed by Darius. Fourteen years passed, and as we will see in the next study, it was not until the spirited preaching of Haggai and Zechariah that the project got back on course.

Unfortunately, the Jews became so discouraged with rebuilding the temple that they turned to building and beautifying their own homes (Hag. 1:4). When we lose the clear focus of spiritual things, other things take their place. God's work must always be more important than our own.

DISCUSSION

When the Jews returned to Judah, they assembled in Jerusalem with a unified purpose. Discuss what that purpose was, what role worship played in them accomplishing it, and what opposition they encountered.

1. If you had been an exiled Jew facing the challenges involved in traveling to Judah, would you have decided to make the long journey? Why or why not?

2. How would you describe the will of the returnees as they gathered in Jerusalem?

3. What factors do you see as major threats to the unity of a local church?

4. Why is it significant that the returnees built the altar before they laid the foundation of the temple?

5. Why do you agree or disagree that God values our worship above our service?

6. Read Romans 12:1–2. What offering can a believer present to God that honors and pleases Him?

7. Read Ezra 3:10–12. Why does the completion of work done scripturally and wholeheartedly lead to praise, thanksgiving, and joy?

8. Based on your reading of Ezra 4:1–5, should believers let unbelievers partner with them in the Lord's work? Why or why not?

PRAYER

Father, help us remember to come before You first as we undertake Your kingdom's work. May we never take a single step without Your guidance.

3

GOD'S PLAN IS NOT DETOURED

Ezra 6:1–3, 13–22

God persists in fulfiilling His plan.

During the construction of the temple in Jerusalem, the Jews had to contend with lots of grit. Hostile neighbors opposed the building project and political pressure delayed it. However, God provided "drops of oil"—the prophets Haggai and Zechariah and the leaders Zerubbabel and Jeshua—to help the project move forward to completion.

This study will help you work smoothly to complete whatever tasks God has assigned to you.

COMMENTARY

When David made plans for building the first temple, he did so from a position of strength. After conquering the neighboring nations, he began to assemble much of the inventory and many of the contractors Solomon would later use for the construction. But when the second temple was built, Israel was far from being a political power. They had to receive permission to go and build the temple from the king of Persia. That permission vacillated with the political wind for about ninety years.

Persia was divided into provinces, each ruled by a governor. Sometimes a governor would notify the king about something the Jews were doing. Other times, local residents would ask their governor to report some accusation to the king. If the king sided with the opposition, then the Jews would be forced to stop the work.

The first recorded incident of harassment was initiated by people who had been moved to Judah. They were not listed in the census in chapter 2. Zerubbabel rejected their offer to help. These people continued to harass the workers for sixteen years (4:5). They hired advisors to make the work more difficult. In addition, Cambyses, the successor to Cyrus, was not a friend of the Jews and granted comfort to their enemies.

The second incident of harassment came during the reign of Artaxerxes. One of his officers, Bishlam (4:7), and his associates wrote a letter to Artaxerxes accusing the Jews of being a "rebellious" and "troublesome" people (4:15). They asked the king to investigate their history. After his investigation, Artaxerxes stopped the work (4:21–24).

The third incident of harassment was led by Tattenai, who was the governor of Coele-Syria and Phoenicia under Darius (5:3–17). The Jews said King Cyrus had made a decree giving them authority to rebuild the temple. To Tattenai's credit, his letter to Darius asked if Cyrus had given the Jews that authority. Chapter 6 is the search and discovery of that decree, and Darius's new decree that allowed the completion of the temple proper.

While we are still in this section describing the hindrances and obstacles, Ezra introduces the prophetic ministries of Haggai and Zechariah (5:1–2). In the midst of harassment, they prophesied in the name of God (5:1) and brought the message of God to the people of God. Although we do not know what they said, the result was that the leaders started rebuilding the temple. The prophets stayed with the workers and helped them.

King Cyrus's Decree (Ezra 6:1–3)

The sixth chapter of Ezra can be divided into two main parts: The decrees of Cyrus and Darius are the focus of the first half (6:1–12); the completion of the temple, the installation of worship, and the way God changed the hearts of the Persian kings completes the second half of the chapter (6:13–22).

> ### WORDS FROM WESLEY
> #### Ezra 6:1
>
> *A decree*—To search the rolls in Babylon, where search was first made; but not finding the edict there, they searched in Achmetha, or Ecbatana, and found it. (ENOT)

King Cyrus's decree was emphatic legislation. The phrases **let the temple be rebuilt** and **let its foundation be laid** (v. 3) are given with intensity. Cyrus's decree had a major effect on Darius. Darius extended all of the essentials of Cyrus's order and added punishment of death for anyone who caused his order to be changed. He prayed for the destruction of any people who would attempt to destroy this temple.

The Temple Is Completed (Ezra 6:13–15)

After Darius issued his decree and it was communicated to Tattenai, the governor completely fulfilled his requirement diligently. In chapter 5, Tattenai questioned the authority for building the temple. Now, the king placed upon him the task of supplying the building materials.

The building program was caused to prosper under the prophetic preaching of Haggai and Zechariah. The people of God considered the command of God as that of the supreme judge, which they diligently obeyed.

> ## WORDS FROM WESLEY
> ### Ezra 6:14
>
> *Through the prophecying*—This is a seasonable intimation that this great and unexpected success was not to be ascribed to chance, or to the kindness or good humour of Darius, but unto God only, who by His prophets had required and encouraged them to proceed in the work, and by His mighty power disposed Darius's heart to such kind and noble purposes. (ENOT)

The decrees of the Persian kings were the law of the land. The Jews looked to Persian law to give them space to function, and they used the power of the law to complete their project. **The temple was completed . . . in the sixth year of the reign of King Darius** (v. 15). Since we know Darius came to power in 522 B.C., we can calculate that the temple was completed in 516 B.C.

Worship at the New Temple (Ezra 6:16–21)

The dedication of the temple was **celebrated . . . with joy** (v. 16). Seventy years after the destruction of Solomon's temple, twenty-two years of which were filled with work and hardship, the new temple to the name of God was completed. In the dedication service, **twelve male goats, one for each** tribe, were offered as a sin offering (v. 17). Israel knew that its last seventy years of captivity were a result of their sin. At the dedication, the divisions of the priests and Levites were installed. Each division worked for fourteen days and was then replaced by the next division.

The exiles celebrated the Passover correctly: correct time, correct preparation, and correct practice.

God Changed the Attitude of the Kings (Ezra 6:22)

The temple was completed by the command of God and the decrees of Cyrus, Darius, and Artaxerxes, kings of Persia (6:14). It is obvious that God changed the hearts of all three of these kings.

Cyrus. Some have questioned the validity of Cyrus, the most powerful ruler in his day, as a person who would rebuild the temple and restore the valuable vessels to the temple. Some scholars think Cyrus restored the deities of previously conquered nations to gain the favor of the captured people. Others think he had more selfish reasons, such as placating foreign gods in order to avoid divine retribution. Whatever his reasoning or motivation, Cyrus dramatically and emphatically changed the course of Jewish history with his order. Conquered and vanquished people typically don't have the core of their faith restored by despots.

Darius. During the reign of Cambyses and the first two years of the reign of Darius, the people rebuilding the temple were being harassed. It was not until Darius found Cyrus's decree that he changed his attitude. He ordered all hindrances to be removed, and he ordered Tattenai to supply all the needs for the construction to be paid from the royal treasury. Darius even prayed for the temple: May God "overthrow any king or people who lift a hand to change this decree or to destroy this temple in Jerusalem" (6:12).

Artaxerxes. Artaxerxes actually stopped the work of the walls of Jerusalem (4:21–24). Some may say that this stoppage was just for building the wall. But a portion of the wall helped to form the court around the temple. Later, when Ezra went to Artaxerxes, he was granted all his requests (7:6).

All three of these Persian kings had a change of attitude.

> ### WORDS FROM WESLEY
> #### Ezra 6:22
>
> *Joyful*—He had given them both cause to rejoice, and hearts to rejoice. God is the fountain whence all the streams of true joy flow. *Of Assyria*—Of the king of Persia, who was now king of Assyria also, here so called emphatically, to note the great power and goodness of God in turning the hearts of these great monarchs, whose predecessors had been the chief persecutors and oppressors of God's people. (ENOT)

Lessons from Ezra

The book of Ezra demonstrates God using political power to fulfill His purposes. It took political power to give authority for the captives to be set free. It took political power to return the valuables stolen from the temple. Since the Jews had been stripped of their wealth and held as slaves, it took political power to fund a project this big.

The return of the captives from exile is another example of our saving God. Just as God remembered Noah during the flood and saved him and his family, just as God remembered His covenant with Abraham while the Jews were in Egyptian captivity and led them forth to the Promised Land, God was restoring His people according to His promises (Jer. 25:12).

When the book begins, the Jewish religion and its core expressions of worship lie in ruins in Jerusalem. In the first six chapters of the book, the temple and its altar are rebuilt and functioning, its priesthood and Levitical systems are reinstalled, its normal practices of worship are reinstituted, and its moral and spiritual life is reformed. The book of Ezra is an example of God renewing, reviving, and rebuilding His people.

Ezra demonstrates the proper use of political power to fulfill God's plan. Haggai and Zechariah and the elders used the building permit Cyrus had given to them. That permit gave them legal grounds to claim their privilege to construct the temple.

The prophetic ministry is also on display in the book of Ezra. Haggai and Zechariah brought the message of God to their congregation. With all of the local and royal opposition, their message had to be informative and inspirational. The prophetic ministry was addressed to a particular person or group, usually God's people. Sometimes it also contained futuristic events. But as we study prophetic truth, we must always look for its original audience.

Ezra describes a place for worship and work in the construction of God's house. Today, churches have groundbreaking services, cornerstone-laying services, and church-dedication services. But Ezra describes a different type of service. As the masons began to lay the foundation stones, some weighing hundreds of thousands of pounds, the priests and Levites, in full vestments, with orchestration and choral presentation, praised God. The dignity and glory of God was linked to the difficult but important work of the construction. The words, melodies, harmonies, and rhythms of praise to God embellished the building of the temple.

Rather than defining faith, Ezra helps us visualize it. As the book begins, the temple and Jerusalem are in ruins, and the Jews are in captivity with no visible symbols and no hope of restoration. Six chapters later, they are in Jerusalem and the temple is built.

Their journey began with the faith of a few people: Zerubbabel, Ezra, Nehemiah, Haggai, Zechariah, and some others. They believed Jeremiah's prophecy of their return. They accepted God's plan as their plan. As they shared their faith, their faith spread to others. Eventually, their faith cost them time, money, sacrifice, and effort. Their faith was challenged by political rulings. But in the sixth year of Darius, the temple was complete. Faith saw what eyes didn't see. Faith turned promises into reality. Faith brought the future into the present.

Ezra also teaches that faith and its achievements are not the end; they are only stepping stones in the plan of God. Years after the temple was rebuilt, reforms and new concepts still needed to be incorporated into God's work with His people.

DISCUSSION

The enemies who opposed the construction of the temple succeeded in halting the work, but only for a time. Under Darius of Persia, a decree was issued that allowed the Jews to resume the construction.

1. What convinced Darius that the temple construction was a duly authorized project?
2. How do you see God's controlling hand in Darius's decree?
3. Read Ezra 6:8–10. How did the decree support the construction effort in practical ways?
4. According to Ezra 6:11, what penalty would befall anyone who violated the king's decree?
5. Read Ezra 6:12. Do you think Darius was a believer in the true God? Why or why not?
6. What attitude accompanied the completion of the temple? How might you increase this attitude in your worship?
7. Read verse 22. Why do you agree or disagree that believers generally need to be more confident that God can change the attitude of a nation's elected officials?
8. How do the events of Ezra 6 encourage you to trust God to handle a difficult situation you are facing?

PRAYER

Father, give us the wisdom to know how to use our political system to further Your kingdom. Help us be wise as serpents and innocent as doves (Matt. 10:16).

4

GOING WHERE GOD IS LEADING

Ezra 7:6–10, 27–28; 8:21–23, 31–32, 35–36

Live under the providential hand of God.

According to the Nielson Company, the average American spends nearly five hours a day watching TV. The habit may be injurious to viewers' health if it keeps them from exercising. We might also argue that excessive TV viewing is injurious to viewers' spiritual health if it keeps them from spending adequate time reading, studying, and meditating upon the Bible. Ezra knew how essential the Scriptures are to a healthy spiritual life. He devoted himself to the study of Scripture. He obeyed its commands, and he taught it to his countrymen.

This study challenges you to respect and read the Bible with an open mind and heart so you will enjoy vigorous spiritual health.

COMMENTARY

Ezra 6 concluded with the completion and dedication of the rebuilt temple under Zerubbabel in 516 B.C., exactly seventy years after its destruction in 586 B.C. Chapter 7 begins some sixty years later. Between chapters 6 and 7, the events of the book of Esther took place. God allowed Esther, a young and orphaned Jewish woman, to become queen of Persia in order to save the Jews in exile from certain annihilation. The Persian Empire had been handed down from Darius I to King Xerxes and now to Xerxes's son, Artaxerxes I.

Almost fifty thousand people had returned to the land of Judah to rebuild the temple in Jerusalem. The rest of the Jews remained in exile in the region of **Babylon**. But God once again moved in the hearts of the king and His people, and Ezra returned to Jerusalem with at least seventeen hundred men, along with women and children (see 8:21). "He had begun his journey from Babylon on the first day of the first month" (7:9) "in the seventh year of the king" (v. 8), that is, on April 8, 458 B.C., and he "arrived in Jerusalem on the first day of the fifth month" (v. 9), on August 4. The arduous journey was nine hundred miles by foot and took four months.

Ezra's Passion (Ezra 7:6–10, 27–28)

Ezra **was a teacher well versed** (knowledgeable, skillful) **in the Law of Moses** (the first five books of the Bible, v. 6). The Hebrew word used for *teacher* literally means a "scribe." The word was used for one who served as a secretary, writer, or for any learned man who was able to read and write. In time it came to mean one who studied and taught the Scriptures. With all the opportunities for learning in Babylon and Persia, Ezra had not chosen to study the stars or literature, for which the Chaldeans were famous. Instead, he chose to study the Word of God.

WORDS FROM WESLEY
Ezra 7:6

Jesus, with Thine o'ershadowing hand,
With Thine almighty favour bless'd,
Thy servants before kings shall stand,
And prosper'd in their just request,
Boldly dispense that gospel-word,
Which builds the temple of the Lord. (PW, vol. 9, 220)

Ezra had devoted himself (literally, "set his heart firmly") **to the study and observance of the Law of the LORD, and to**

teaching its decrees and laws in Israel (v. 10). From early on, Ezra had purposely and intentionally committed himself to being a man of one book. He studied, obeyed, and taught it.

Jewish tradition holds that it was Ezra who instituted the synagogue form of worship, centered on Scripture and prayer, that flourished during the time of exile when the Jews were unable to worship at the temple in Jerusalem. Tradition also holds that Ezra was the one who first gathered into one edition the books of the Old Testament canon (the books believed to be the authoritative Word of God). Many scholars believe he wrote Psalm 119, extolling the Word of God.

Ezra's passion for God's Word was remarkable. And it didn't go unnoticed by God. Verses 6 and 9 remind us, **for the hand of the Lord his God was on him**; **for the gracious hand of his God was on him** (compare 7:28; 8:18, 22, 31; Neh. 2:8, 18). It was God who put the passion in Ezra's heart. It was God who led him. It was God who protected him. It was God who granted him favor before the king. Ezra was passionate about the Word of God because, ultimately, he had a passion for the God of the Word. When Ezra put God's interests first, God responded with favor and granted him success in all he put his hand to.

Ezra's Praise (Ezra 7:27–28)

In verses 27 and 28, we find the first use of the first person in Ezra, indicating that these words were part of his memoirs and were inserted verbatim. These are the words of Ezra himself as he penned them. And it is significant that they are words of praise: **Praise be to the Lord, the God of our fathers** (v. 27). The word for *praise* (Hebrew, *baruch*) literally means "blessed," a popular opening word in many Jewish prayers. Here Ezra blessed or praised God for moving the heart of the king to bring God honor **in this way**. Ezra had just received the letter from King Artaxerxes (7:12–26) granting him permission to return to

Judah with his fellow Jews and giving him gold, silver, and all the monies he needed to supply the temple and to purchase offerings to sacrifice to the Lord. The letter also excluded those who served in the temple from paying taxes. Artaxerxes commissioned Ezra to appoint magistrates and judges over Judah, to teach the people the Word of God, and to severely punish those who refused to obey God's law. The king's decrees would **bring honor to** (literally, "glorify") **the house of the LORD** (v. 27). Why would a pagan king treat God's house and law with such respect? It wasn't just his desire to win the favor of another culture's god. It wasn't simply because of the powerful witness of dedicated men like Ezra. It was because God had **put it into the king's heart**. There is no one outside God's realm of authority, not even the king of the great Persian Empire. "The kings of the earth belong to God" (Ps. 47:9); He is the "God of gods and the Lord of kings" (Dan. 2:47). Ezra understood that it was God alone who should receive praise for the king's favor, because it was all God's doing.

Ezra praised God for moving the heart of the king and also for being gracious to him personally. He acknowledged that God **extended his good favor to** him (v. 28) by the king's and officials' favorable treatment of him, and that **the hand of the LORD his God was on** him. Ezra realized that every blessing was ultimately from the Lord (see James 1:17). And he gave God the praise, glory, and thanksgiving.

Because Ezra saw God's hand at work in all the events taking place, he **took courage and gathered leading men from Israel to go** (v. 28) with him to Jerusalem. Notice that Ezra referred to the Jewish exiles as Israel, rather than Judah, as the author also does in verse 10. Ezra saw Judah (the southern tribes of Judah and Benjamin, which had gone into exile in 586 B.C., the northern ten tribes having been previously exiled by Assyria in 722) as the embodiment of all Israel, and there is little doubt that every tribe was represented by at least a few families.

Ezra 7:6–10, 27–28; 8:21–23, 31–32, 35–36

> ### WORDS FROM WESLEY
> *Ezra 7:28*
>
> If God gives us His hand, we are bold and chearful: if He withdraws it, we are weak as water. Whatever service we are enabled to do for God and our generation, God must have all the glory of it. (ENOT)

Ezra's Petition (Ezra 8:21–23)

En route to Jerusalem, Ezra and his fellow Jews stopped by the **Ahava Canal** (v. 21, location unknown), where they rested for three days (8:15). Ezra proclaimed **a fast, so that we might humble ourselves before our God and ask him for a safe journey for us and our children with all our possessions** (v. 21). Fasting, going without food for a specified period of time, was an indication of earnestness before the Lord and dependence upon Him (compare Neh. 1:4; Dan. 9:3; Matt. 17:21; Acts 14:23). It was an act of humility. Here the band of returning exiles fasted and prayed for God's safety in their travels. They were traveling with women, children, and all their possessions. They would have been an easy—and likely—target for robbers and thieves along the way. Unlike Nehemiah, who traveled this same road thirteen years later with an armed escort, Ezra **was ashamed to ask the king for soldiers** (v. 22) to protect them on their journey. They had witnessed to the king about the graciousness of their God: **The gracious hand of our God is on everyone who looks to him**. After having testified to God's ability to keep them safe, Ezra felt it would dishonor the Lord (and shame them) to ask for the king's protection. It's one thing to proclaim the power of God; it's another to trust and act on it! As they began their travels, no doubt they became uneasy and fearful. It was time to stop and pray: **So we fasted and petitioned our God about this, and he answered our prayer** (v. 23). For three days they fasted and prayed. And God was faithful. "The hand of our God was on us, and he protected us from enemies and bandits along the way" (8:31). He kept them safe until they arrived in Jerusalem (8:32).

WORDS FROM WESLEY
Ezra 8:21

A fast—For public mercies. Public prayers must be made, that all who are to share in the comfort, may share in the requests for it. *Afflict ourselves*—For our sins; and so be qualified for the pardon of them. When we are entering on any new condition of life, our care should be, to bring into it none of the guilt of the sins of our former condition. When we are in any imminent danger, let us make our peace with God, and then nothing can hurt us. *Right way*—A safe and prosperous journey; such a way and course as might be best for us. (ENOT)

No wonder God looked on Ezra with such favor! He was not afraid to proclaim the truth of what he knew about God, even though he struggled when it came to putting it into practice. He knew God's Word was true and trustworthy. And he fasted and prayed until he had the conviction that it was true for him.

Ezra's Priority (Ezra 8:35–36)

After arriving in Jerusalem and resting for three days (8:32), Ezra got right down to business. He wasn't there to renew acquaintances or find family members. Worshiping his God in His temple was his first priority. Remember, Ezra was a Levite in the line of Aaron. This was his destiny; and yet living in exile, he had never had the opportunity to even see, let alone serve in, God's temple. He and the other exiles brought their **burnt offerings** (signifying their dedication to the Lord; see Lev. 1) and their **sin offering** (to atone for their sins; see Lev. 4) to the temple (Ezra 8:35). Notice that they offered **twelve bulls for all Israel**—one for each tribe (see comment on 7:28). In total, they sacrificed twelve bulls, **ninety-six rams, seventy-seven male lambs,** and **twelve male goats,** far fewer than the offerings given by Zerubbabel and the people of Israel at the dedication of the temple in 6:17. But there were also far fewer people with Ezra than there had been with Zerubbabel, so the offering was appropriate. In the law of Moses, God had commanded that His people bring sacrifices, and so they did. Ezra's first act here in 8:35 was an acknowledgment that worshiping God and obeying His Word were his highest priorities.

WORDS FROM WESLEY
Ezra 8:35

Sin offering—For it is the atonement that secures every mercy to us, which will not be truly comfortable, unless iniquity be taken away, and our peace made with God. They offer twelve bullocks, twelve he-goats, and ninety six rams (eight times twelve), signifying the union of the two kingdoms. They did not any longer go two tribes one way, and ten tribes another; but all the twelve met by their representatives at the same altar. (ENOT)

Ezra **also delivered the king's orders to the royal satraps and to the governors** (v. 36) in order to begin the process of fulfilling his mission in Judah. And so, the satraps and governors **gave assistance to the people and to the house of God,** as the king had commanded. In the remainder of the book, Ezra was faithful to teach the people God's law as it pertained to intermarriage (ch. 9), and he led them in confession of their sin and in making a covenant with God to do what was right (10:1–4). Ezra was there for a purpose, and he was diligent about pursuing it. His priority never changed.

DISCUSSION

The Jews had constructed the temple in Jerusalem and reinstituted Levitical worship, but they needed a teacher of the law to help them worship and live properly. Ezra arrived in Jerusalem as their divinely appointed teacher.

1. Why did King Artaxerxes give Ezra everything he asked for?

2. How might believers today discern the hand of God on a pastor or other spiritual leader?

3. How important was God's Word in Ezra's life? Do you agree or disagree that, above all other pursuits, pastors should devote themselves to the Word of God?

4. Read Acts 6:3–4. How can you and your fellow believers help your pastor(s) spend more time in Bible study and prayer?

5. How can you devote more time to Bible study and prayer?

6. Ezra was also a man of praise (Ezra 7:27–28). Suggest at least three reasons every Christian should praise the Lord.

7. En route from Babylon to Jerusalem, why did Ezra stop for a while to fast and pray?

8. Ezra's handling of finances was above reproach (Ezra 8:24–30). How can a church handle its finances in a manner that is above reproach?

PRAYER

Father, give us a passion to study Your Word, to know it, and to teach it. Guide us as we dig deeper into Your truth.

5

HANDLING GOD-GIVEN BURDENS
Nehemiah 1:1–11; 2:4–5, 11–12, 17–18

A burden from God drives us to prayer then action.

Have you ever asked your boss for a really big favor, like a large raise or extra time off? Imagine if the boss had the power to execute you if he or she felt offended. Nehemiah asked his boss, the king of Persia, to grant him time off to rebuild Jerusalem. But before talking to the king, he talked to God.

You cannot have success in any venture unless God grants it. Follow Nehemiah's example and trust God to give you success.

COMMENTARY

Even though Cyrus, king of Persia, legally granted the opportunity to return to Judah, many of the Jews living in exile chose to remain there. Many had been born there and were fully integrated into the society. In this dispersed Jewish community in exile, Nehemiah lived and served in the Persian court in a very high capacity some 140 years after the 586 B.C. destruction of Jerusalem.

Nehemiah's Request for News Regarding Jerusalem (Neh. 1:1–3)

Much of the book of Nehemiah is written in a first-person autobiographical style (referred to as Nehemiah's memoirs: 1:1–7:73; 12:27–13:31), which is introduced in the opening words of the book: **The words of Nehemiah** (1:1).

The account begins **in the month of Kislev**, which would be November-December, **in the twentieth year**, which is most likely the same as "the twentieth year of King Artaxerxes" specified in

2:1. It is generally accepted that this is Artaxerxes I (464–424 B.C.), which places these events in 445 B.C.

Nehemiah was residing in **Susa**, a Persian city located about 150 miles north of where the Tigris and Euphrates Rivers flow into the Persian Gulf.

As cupbearer (1:11), Nehemiah's primary responsibility was to choose and taste the wine before serving it to the king to assure that it was poison-free. Persons holding that position were highly regarded, and other responsibilities of authority and governmental administration were delegated to them. Indeed, Nehemiah was given the administrative appointment of governor over Judah during his twelve-year tenure there (5:14; 12:26).

Upon the arrival of the group of men from Judah, it was Nehemiah who inquired of them (**I questioned them**, v. 2). Nehemiah's inquiry, and subsequently the response given to him, was twofold in nature, relating to (1) the welfare of the people residing there (**the Jewish remnant that survived the exile**), and (2) the physical condition of the city (**and also about Jerusalem**).

Those who survived the exile and are back in the province (v. 3) probably refers to both the descendants of the original group of returnees in approximately 538 B.C. as well as to the newer returnees who had immigrated back to Judah. They were described to Nehemiah as being **in great trouble** and suffering **disgrace**, both of which are tied to the reality that the **wall of Jerusalem is broken down and its gates have been burned with fire**. The city's ruined condition describes the situation that it had been in for the previous 140 years. But a more recent event may have motivated Nehemiah's inquiry. Ezra 4:7–23 recounts that during the reign of Artaxerxes, opposition to the rebuilding of the city wall had been voiced, and that Artaxerxes had decreed the cessation of any rebuilding efforts (4:21). Those efforts were then quashed by force (4:23).

Nehemiah's Response to the News (Neh. 1:4)

When Nehemiah heard the news, it had a deep impact upon him. First, he **sat down and wept** and **mourned** (v. 4), which reflected an attitude of contrition. Mourning involved not only weeping or just an inward attitude, but also outward gestures such as tearing one's garment, putting on sackcloth, and putting dust and ashes on one's head (compare Neh. 9:1; Ezra 9:3–5). The weeping and mourning were also accompanied by **fasting** and **praying** (Neh. 1:4).

Nehemiah's Prayer (Neh. 1:5–11)

Nehemiah's prayer sequentially moves through three main parts: invocation (vv. 5–6), confession (vv. 6–7), and petition (vv. 8–11).

Invocation (Neh. 1:5). The invocation helps to properly orient one's focus by addressing the prayer to God and reciting qualities and attributes of God that serve as the bases for the subsequent confession and requests. This particular ascription extols and praises God as **Lord** and **God of heaven**.

The emphasis on the covenant relationship between God and His people is highlighted in the last line of the ascription: He **keeps his covenant of love with those who love him and obey his commands** (v. 5). This summarizes the twofold aspect involved in the divine-human interchange in the covenant relationship. The divine side is characterized by love (sometimes translated "steadfast love" or "lovingkindness"). Once the covenant relationship has been established by virtue of Yahweh's loving actions toward His people (see Deut. 7:8–9; 10:15), then the response on the part of the people is to love God in return and to observe the commands He has given to them (see Deut. 6:5–6; 10:12–13; 11:1).

Confession (Neh. 1:6–7). In this confession, the acknowledgment of sin is emphasized through the accumulation of three different general terms for sinning (vv. 6–7: **sins, acted wickedly, not obeyed**; compare a similar threefold accumulation in 1 Kings 8:47; 2 Chron. 6:37). Those covenant transgressions are described in three ways: (1) they have sinned against God (**the sins we ... have committed against you**, Neh. 1:6); (2) they have acted wickedly toward God (**we have acted very wickedly toward you**, v. 7); and (3) they have not kept God's commands (**we have not obeyed the commands, decrees and laws you gave**, v. 7).

The situation for which Nehemiah was praying is one of national magnitude, and so he acted as an intercessor on behalf of the nation and confessed the sins of the community that had led to those consequences (**I confess the sins we Israelites ... have committed**, v. 6). But as an intercessor, Nehemiah did not distance and separate himself from the people, confessing only what "they" had done. He acknowledged his part and responsibility in contributing to the situation of judgment and confessed his personal sins and the sins of his ancestry and household (**I confess the sins we Israelites, including myself and my father's house**, v. 6).

Petition (Neh. 1:6, 8–11). The petitions in the prayer are of three kinds. First is the initial petition in verse 6 that God would hear the prayer: **Let your ear be attentive and your eyes open to hear the prayer your servant is praying before you**, which is repeated in verse 11. The beginning and ending repetition stresses that Nehemiah truly desired a receptive and favorable hearing from the Lord.

The second petition is found in verses 8–9. Nehemiah asked God to **remember** a couple of the specific covenant blessings and curses.

Within the covenant relationship, whether the people received the blessings was contingent upon their obedience to God (as already indicated in v. 5): if the people were obedient, then they would receive the blessings; if the people were disobedient, then they would suffer the consequences of God's punishment (that is, the curses; see Deut. 11:26–28).

There was no question that God had, in the past, been faithful to the specific covenant curse of the exile (Neh. 1:8) in that He did bring the punishment as He said He would. Nehemiah was now requesting that God be faithful to the "blessing" aspect of His covenant word as expressed in verse 9, specifically by gathering and returning His people to the land.

WORDS FROM WESLEY
Nehemiah 1:11

To fear thy name—Those who truly desire to fear His name, shall be graciously accepted of God. *This man*—The king: who is but a man and therefore his heart is wholly at thy disposal. Favour with men is then comfortable, when we see it springing from the mercy of God. (ENOT)

Nehemiah's Request of the King (Neh. 2:4–5)

According to 2:1, after four months had passed (**Nisan** is March or April), the occasion arose for Nehemiah to address his request to the king. While Nehemiah served wine to the king, the king noticed the sadness of Nehemiah's countenance (v. 2). The king asked Nehemiah what was troubling him (v. 2). Once Nehemiah expressed what was troubling him (v. 3), the king then asked what Nehemiah wanted to do in light of the circumstances (v. 4: **What is it you want?**).

Prior to responding to the king, Nehemiah declared, **"Then I prayed to the God of heaven"** (v. 4). Clearly this was not an audible or long prayer, but rather a short, silent one that was concise and directly to the point.

After the quick prayer, Nehemiah deferentially acknowledged that the decision was the king's and was based on what pleased the king (**If it pleases the king and if your servant has found favor in his sight**, v. 5). Yet, as Nehemiah's prayer of chapter 1 reflects, Nehemiah understood that it was ultimately a matter of what God decided to do and not something that lay solely with the human king's prerogative. The broad contours of Nehemiah's requested plan were then made known to the king: **Let him send me to the city . . . so that I can rebuild it** (v. 5).

In verses 3 and 5, by speaking of the ruined condition of **the city where** his **fathers** were **buried**, Nehemiah diplomatically presented his request as a matter of personal relevance and concern rather than as a politically significant situation. He did not express it in terms of refortifying the city, nor did he mention that the city was Jerusalem.

WORDS FROM WESLEY
Nehemiah 2:4–5

My sadness comes not from any disaffection to the king, for whom my hearty prayers are that he may live for ever; but from another cause. *Sepulchres*—Which by all nations are esteemed sacred and inviolable. He saith not a word of the temple as he spake before a heathen king who cared for none of these things. *I prayed*—To direct my thoughts and words, and to incline the king's heart to grant my request. (ENOT)

Nehemiah's responses to the king's questions (vv. 5–8) show that he had thought through precisely how to respond, even to the point of detailed preplanning. First, he gave an estimated time of how long he would be gone (v. 6). Second, he requested letters from the king (v. 7) showing that he was on a royally commissioned enterprise so as to assure safe conduct. Nehemiah also probably anticipated a negative reaction to the restarting of the building project (see 2:9–10), so these official documents likely gave him royal authority, which reversed the previous decree. Third, Nehemiah requested letters acquisitioning the necessary building materials (v. 8), not only for the city wall, but also for his personal residence. He had thought through even the specifics related to the construction needs of the project.

Nehemiah's Private Surveying of the Ruins (Neh. 2:11–12)

There is a time lapse of **three days** (v. 11) between Nehemiah's arrival and the revealing of his plans to the people.

In conducting a personal examination of the ruined city wall, the intent of such was clearly not to ascertain whether the project was feasible. Nehemiah fully intended to rebuild the wall as expressed in the conviction of verse 12: **what my God had put in my heart to do for Jerusalem.** The survey was rather for Nehemiah to get a firsthand look to assess the damage, which would enable him to further formulate how to go about the rebuilding. This survey was done in the secrecy of the darkness of night (**I set out during the night**, v. 12) and without informing the local leadership of his intentions (vv. 3, 16). Nehemiah's intentional concealment of his plan prevented the opposition from having an opportunity to attempt to preemptively stop the work before it began.

WORDS FROM WESLEY
Nehemiah 2:12

Night—Concealing both his intentions as long as he could, knowing that the life of his business lay in secrecy and expedition. *Beast*—To prevent noise. (ENOT)

Nehemiah's Enlistment of the People (Neh. 2:17–18)

Verses 17–18 do not specify whether this was a general assembly or a more private meeting with just officials and representatives.

But it was shortly after Nehemiah's night survey. Nehemiah tactfully cited the condition that the city was in, which they themselves would surely verify: **You see the trouble we are in: Jerusalem lies in ruins, and its gates have been burned with fire** (v. 17). He then moved to an exhortation to action: **Come, let us rebuild the wall of Jerusalem and we will no longer be in disgrace** (v. 17).

In verse 18, Nehemiah bore witness that this was a divinely sanctioned work: **I . . . told them about the gracious hand of my God upon me and what the king had said to me.** The implication was that since God's hand had been upon the project up to that point, God would see that the project would be successfully completed (compare the explicit declaration of such in 2:20).

Once Nehemiah had given the exhortation with the motivations, the people wholeheartedly responded: **Let us start rebuilding** (v. 18). And the project began: **So they began this good work** (v. 18, literally, "They strengthened their hands for this good thing"). The reference to both God's hand and the people's hands in verse 18 indicates a coordinated effort (compare also 2:8).

WORDS FROM WESLEY

Nehemiah 2:18

Rise up—Let us do it with vigour and diligence and resolution, as those that are determined to go through with it. (ENOT)

Nehemiah 1:1–11; 2:4–5, 11–12, 17–18

DISCUSSION

As you study this study's Scripture passages, see how God used Nehemiah in his position, and consider how He can use you where He has placed you.

1. Why was Nehemiah's position so important to the king? Who is counting on you to do your work faithfully?

2. How did Nehemiah show compassion? How did he show honesty? How did he show confidence in God?

3. What conditions do you find most disturbing about our nation? How do express your concern? What are you asking God to accomplish in our nation?

4. Why were strong walls in Jerusalem a major concern to Nehemiah?

5. Why do you agree or disagree that a congregation should do its best to maintain a safe and attractive church building?

6. How can Nehemiah's prayer serve as a model for prayer today?

7. Why is it so important to petition God before requesting a favor of some human in authority?

8. What principles of leadership do you learn from the way Nehemiah approached the challenge of rebuilding Jerusalem's walls?

PRAYER

Father, we look to You as the author and finisher of the work You have called us to do. Help our hands join with Yours in all we undertake.

6

VICTORY IN ADVERSITY

Nehemiah 4:1–15, 19–20

Work together with God to resist adversity.

Discouragement is one of the Devil's most effective tools. As doubts bombard our faith, we fail to assume our share of God's work. "It will never work," we say. Or we ask, "What's the use of trying?" We hand the Devil victory on a silver platter.

Nehemiah did not let discouragement destroy the work of rebuilding Jerusalem's walls. He prayed, organized and armed the workers, and established a vigilant guard. He would not accept failure.

As this study teaches, you should not grow weary in the work of the Lord. In due season, you will reap if you do not give up.

COMMENTARY

Nehemiah was a unique, godly layman who had outstanding organizational skills and gave meticulous attention to details. As the people began the work of repairing and rebuilding the wall, he wisely assigned households to work in family groups. In the same way, the starting point for every Christian's kingdom work is his or her home and neighborhood.

Chapter 3 shows how people of every status and level of society can be used in God's work. There is a place of ministry for every person who is willing to work. Once we start, God often brings outsiders to help carry the load (Neh. 4:2, 5, 7). As momentum builds, some are willing to take on more than their fair share, even beyond the call of duty (vv. 11, 19, 21). This story shows wonderful cooperation. It also teaches that not everyone will work and cooperate, even some who are known as leaders (v. 5).

The opening verse tells us the leaders dedicated this building project to the Lord. This enormous task required great organization and diligent work. However, Nehemiah realized this was primarily a spiritual mission. The events of chapter 4 remind us that any work done for God will become the target of Satan's strong opposition.

Facing Satan's Opposition (Neh. 4:1-3)

Throughout human history when people have attempted to do great things for God, Satan has formed a plan of attack to try to stop them. For decades, Jerusalem's walls laid in neglect and ruin. This despicable situation was an ugly symbol of Satan's supremacy over God's chosen people. So when Nehemiah came up with a plan to rebuild and restore, Satan immediately mobilized men to mount a defensive attack.

Sanballat and Tobiah had enjoyed free rein to dominate the people of Jerusalem and the surrounding areas. They wanted to continue this position that allowed them to exploit and control the people and reap the profits involved. A number of trade routes passed through that section, and these rulers had a monopoly. While that was their earthly motivation, they were also unwitting pawns in the hand of God's archenemy, Satan. The ways of Satan are cunning and deceitful, but not new.

Tactics of the Enemy (Neh. 4:1-3, 7-8, 10-12, 15)

Ridicule and Mockery (Neh. 4:1-3). In the story of Nehemiah, we see weapons common in Satan's arsenal. As the enemy leaders saw the amazing progress in the rebuilding of the walls, they reached in and pulled out the dagger of ridicule and mockery. **When Sanballat heard . . . he ridiculed the Jews, and in the presence of his associates and the army of**

Samaria, he said, "What are these feeble Jews doing? Will they restore their wall? Will they finish in a day? Can they bring the stones back to life from those heaps of rubble—burned as they are?" (vv. 1–2). Tobiah twisted the knife even deeper as he scornfully mocked, **"What they are building—if even a fox climbed up on it, he would break down their wall of stones!"** (v. 3).

It would appear Sanballat brought an entire army of Samaritans to stand around and gawk at Nehemiah's recruits as they worked. These evil leaders knew the king of Persia had authorized and financed this massive project. Because of this, it was highly unlikely that they would mount any military attack. Yet Sanballat and Tobiah hoped their ridicule and mocking would intimidate and sidetrack the volunteers, thus hindering the completion of the wall. These initial efforts did not succeed, for the people continued to work wholeheartedly (v. 6).

Threats of Violence (Neh. 4:7–8, 15). When the walls continued to go up, the enemy reacted again, this time with intense anger (v. 7). These troublemakers formed an alliance and influenced many from the surrounding areas to join them in threatening the people of God. Their plan of action was to make a big show of military power without carrying out a direct attack. No doubt these conniving cohorts feared the authority of the monarch Artaxerxes. Yet they spread stories of a planned attack, hoping the threats to kill would cause the workers to cower to inactivity, bringing the work to a halt.

However, these threats of violence did not gain success. Once the knowledge of the evil plan reached Nehemiah and his people, the element of surprise vanished, and the threat was largely ended (v. 15).

Threats of violence against God's workers can often inflict impending fear. Satan knows if he can plant fear in the hearts of Christians, he has a chance to impede their effectiveness. Knowing and trusting God will allow us to rise above the violent threats of Satan.

Discouragement and Despair (Neh. 4:10–12). The tired workers began to address their situation in what they felt was a realistic assessment. Discouragement comes when people are tired. Despair was creeping in. They began to cry out, **"The strength of the laborers is giving out, and there is so much rubble that we cannot rebuild the wall"** (v. 10). The ridicule and fear were taking an emotional toll on the people who had worked so hard. Now they began to feel the fatigue and forecasted the workers would run out of strength.

WORDS FROM WESLEY
Nehemiah 4:12

Tho' these had not zeal enough to help in the work, yet they had some concern for their brethren. *Ten times*—Very often. A certain number for an uncertain. *Be upon you*—They will invade you every way, by which we can come to you or you to us; therefore keep watches on every side. (ENOT)

The people of Judah quoted rumors of what their enemies were reported to be saying: **"Before they** [the Jews] **know it or see us, we will be right there among them and will kill them and put an end to the work"** (v. 11). Discouragement drops us to the low level of listening to hearsay. Once they began listening to rambling rumors regarding the enemy, they became open to the viewpoint of their nonbelieving neighbors. **Then the Jews who lived near them came and told us ten times over, "Wherever you turn, they will attack us"** (v. 12).

We see the insidious progression of discouragement. When we're on a wave of momentum and no troubles come, it seems that nothing can deter or defeat us. If Satan attacks when we're tired, then despair and discouragement down us. Next, we listen to hearsay and begin believing the tales of tragedy to come.

Turning Back the Enemy (Neh. 4:4–15, 19–20)

This vivid story of the strategy of the opposition could leave us as cowards with no place to run. However, as we carefully examine the responses of Nehemiah, we learn how we can be victorious over Satan's opposition.

Persistent Prayer (Neh. 4:4–6, 9). Nehemiah was a man of prayer. When Sanballat and his allies ridiculed and mocked the nation of Israel, the immediate response of Nehemiah was prayer: **"Hear us, O our God, for we are despised. . . . They have thrown insults in the face of the builders!"** (4:4–5). When the enemy mounted threats of violence, Nehemiah responded with prayer (v. 9).

WORDS FROM WESLEY

Nehemiah 4:5

Cover not—Let their wickedness be in thy sight, so as to bring down judgments upon them, that either they may be reformed, or others may be warned by their example. God is said to cover or hide sin when he forbears to punish it. *Provoked thee*—They have not only provoked us builders, but thee also. (ENOT)

Once Nehemiah and the people had committed to God the jeering scoffs and threats of the enemy, they were able to keep right on working: **So we rebuilt the wall till all of it reached half its height, for the people worked with all their heart** (v. 6). Prayer and work go hand in hand. There is no better way to rise above ridicule and mocking than to develop a lifestyle of persistent prayer.

Watchful Vigilance (Neh. 4:9, 13). The people of Judah did not take lightly the threats of the enemy. Nehemiah placed priority in prayer but realized the situation called for action as well. **But we prayed to our God and posted a guard day and night to meet this threat** (v. 9). Nehemiah carefully studied the dangers and developed a defensive plan. **Therefore I stationed some of the people behind the lowest points of the wall at the exposed places, posting them by families, with their swords, spears and bows** (v. 13). He posted guards at the points of greatest vulnerability, having families stand guard together. Nehemiah knew the people would be motivated to protect their own. He organized the workers in alternating shifts of sentinel duty; half stood guard while the other half worked. Those who carried building materials and supplies were instructed to keep a weapon in one hand (vv. 16–17). He also ordered all the workers to stay inside the city at night to beef up the security force. The builders slept in their clothes and even carried a weapon when they fetched water (vv. 21–23). He wanted the people to be aware and alert at all times.

Encouragement and Comfort (Neh. 4:14). Nehemiah was a people person. He knew the value of encouragement and comfort when circumstances have stretched people's strength to the limit. God uses these to help people who are pressed and discouraged by despairing situations. Note Nehemiah's skillful ways of bringing encouragement. **Don't be afraid of them. Remember the Lord, who is great and awesome** (v. 14).

WORDS FROM WESLEY
Nehemiah 4:14

Looked—He looked up, engaged God for him, and put himself and his cause under the Divine protection. That was his way, and should be ours: all his cares, all his griefs, all his fears he spread before God. *Great and terrible*—You think your enemies are great and terrible. But what are they in comparison of God? Especially in opposition to Him. (ENOT)

Carefully study the methods of this marvelous mentor. Throughout his story, we see astute observation; he examined each situation for the minutest details. He spoke a message of encouragement and comfort, then called them to remember the Lord's great power. As we focus on the sovereign Lord, the almighty God, courage replaces our despair. When we clearly understand the majesty and might of God, we are no longer immobilized by fear. We can turn back the enemy and neutralize his influence by giving encouragement and comfort.

Armaments and Organization (Neh. 4:16–20). Nehemiah prayed, watched, and gave comfort to his workers. However, he also gave attention to armaments and organization. He was proactive in his plan to build the wall. He also reacted to the enemy's threats by devising a defensive plan. This plan shows Nehemiah's extraordinary organizational skills. He refused to lose sight of the mission, and kept on building the walls (v. 6). Responding to the dangers, he posted guards twenty-four hours a day (v. 9). He stationed sentinels at the most vulnerable spots along the wall. He grouped the guarding forces by families, challenging them to protect their beloved relatives (vv. 13–14). He equipped them adequately with swords, spears, and bows (vv. 13, 16). He positioned the ranking officers at strategic posts. There they could see the enemy and apprise the workers of impending danger and issue orders for counterattack (v. 16). Nehemiah also designed a rallying plan. The distance of the wall work spanned several miles, separating the recruits. The people were instructed to run toward the sound of the trumpet (vv. 19–20).

Nehemiah confidently expected God to help them face the opposition through persistent prayer, watchful vigilance, encouraging comfort, armaments, and organization. With all these weapons in hand, ready to use, he could say with assurance, **"Our God will fight for us!"** (v. 20).

DISCUSSION

As you read Nehemiah 4, discover how organizational skills and reliance on God gain victory over adversity.

1. Why did Nehemiah and the builders of Jerusalem's walls face adversity?

2. How would you describe the first assault Sanballat and Tobiah launched against the builders? Have you ever been a target of a similar assault? If so, what was it, and why was it launched against you?

3. How did the builders respond to the first assault (vv. 4–6)? Why was this response appropriate?

4. Why do you agree or disagree that the devil assaults God's people more vigorously when he sees the work of God succeeding?

5. What threat from within the ranks of the builders do you find in verses 10–12? Why do some Christians become discouraged in the work of the Lord?

6. Read 1 Corinthians 15:58 and Galatians 6:9. How do these verses motivate you to keep on serving God in spite of adversity?

7. Do you agree that "work, watch, and pray" are wise instructions for all who serve the Lord? Why or why not?

8. Read Nehemiah 4:14 and Philippians 1:27–28. Why should believers not fear their adversaries?

PRAYER

Father, when we face the Enemy, let our hearts seek You first. Then grant us wisdom to overcome the Enemy and complete Your work.

FIGHTINGS WITHIN
Nehemiah 5:1–13

Church and personal spiritual growth require complete obedience to God's will.

Many people cannot seem to climb out of debt. Some struggle just to pay monthly interest on their credit cards. For some, their financial problems eventually sap the bliss out of their marriage, so they end up in a divorce court.

Debt and exorbitant interest rates threatened the fabric of life in Judah and challenged Nehemiah to forge a solution. This study can help you understand the dangers of runaway debt.

COMMENTARY

Nehemiah, living in a comfortable city with a secure job, heard of the trouble and disgrace of his people in Jerusalem. The walls and gates were in ruinous condition, so Nehemiah began to fast and pray.

Then he shared his burden and deep concern with his boss, who happened to be the king. The king sent Nehemiah on a fact-finding trip with a big bag of money to do the job. He surveyed the wall in the middle of the night and quickly moved into action. Almost immediately, opposition reared its ugly head.

Nehemiah assigned family groups to work together on different sections of the wall. People from every level of society rolled up their sleeves and worked. Goldsmiths and farmers worked with perfume makers and governors to rebuild the ruined walls. Not everyone got involved, but the majority was motivated to mix mortar and see the stones go up.

The local thugs realized a healthy Jerusalem would spell the end of their exploitation. They did everything possible to deter this visiting leader. They used ridicule and threats. Soon the volunteers were in the depths of discouragement and despair. Nehemiah called the people to pray, remember God, and be united. He called them to hard work, long hours, and constant alertness.

The Problem of Debt (Neh. 5:1–5)

The threats of Sanballat weakened the morale of the Jewish people. They were tired and discouraged. Murmuring accelerated into a loud outcry. Nehemiah had been busy leading the project. Now the talk he heard grabbed his full attention. The wealthier Jews were taking advantage of the poorer people. Three realities threatened to sabotage the work of restoration: hunger, debt, and taxes. The long hours of masonry work left little time to farm or forage for food. The people had large families and the famine exhausted their pantries. They were tired and hungry. People can't work effectively when they are hungry.

Further revelations came out. In the face of famine, poor people had mortgaged their homes and vineyards in exchange for food. Now they were deep in debt. The Persian government required taxes, the straw that strained them to the breaking point. Some of the richer Jews who managed to stay solvent through the hardships loaned money to their starving neighbors, charging unfair interest (usury). The record tells they charged 1 percent each month, or 12 percent per annum (v. 11). Interest piled up on interest soon pushed many into a hopeless pit of debt. This went on so long that some actually sold their children into slavery in order to eat and pay their debts and taxes. They were caught in a vicious cycle.

Debt is a troubling taskmaster. As interest compounds, the repayment is harder to make month after month. Back in the days of Moses, God had forbidden the Jews to charge interest to their own people (see Deut. 23:19–20).

Greed is a strong element of human nature. God knows that. He set forth this law to counteract greed. Now, after the exile when people needed to stand together, they transgressed God's command. In the midst of this project to restore the walls of Jerusalem, Nehemiah had a huge problem to solve. This was probably his greatest test. This sterling leader could have lost the entire cause at this crucial moment. The effort to rebuild could have ended right then in failure.

> ### WORDS FROM WESLEY
> *Nehemiah 5:5*
>
> *Our flesh*—We are of the same nature, and religion with them, though they treat us as if we were beasts or heathens. *Bondage*—We are compelled to sell them for our subsistence. *Daughters*—Which was an evidence of their great necessity, because their daughters were more tender and weak and unfit for bond-service, and more exposed to injuries than their sons. *Redeem*—Which we are allowed to do, but have not wherewith to do it. (ENOT)

The Pattern of Leadership (Neh. 5:6–8)

Nehemiah was a true leader. As he faced this great crisis, we can see convincing qualities of a great leader. He became **angry** (v. 6) about the evil actions of the upper class Jews. Sometimes the only way problems in society can be solved is for leaders to get concerned enough that their hearts boil up in anger. For anger to be righteous, it must lead to remedial action. Jesus saw the moneychangers practicing their evil business in the temple. They were exploiting the worshipers. Jesus became downright angry, but His anger led Him to action. With a whip, He drove out the wrongdoers; He cleaned up the temple, restoring it to its sacred purpose, a house of prayer.

Next, Nehemiah pondered the predicament. Throughout this book, we see examples of this leader who thoughtfully studied the problems he faced. In our fast-paced way of life, we frequently fail to take time to think. Our daily quiet time brings rich benefit. When we pray and listen to God, those moments of communion are also moments of thought. Some of our greatest thoughts and ideas come while we are praying (listening) to God. Nehemiah was a man of prayer, but he was also a man of thought and contemplation.

WORDS FROM WESLEY
Nehemiah 5:7

Exact—Which was against the plain and positive law of God, especially in this time of public calamity. *I set*—I called a public congregation, both of the rulers and people, the greatest part whereof were free from this guilt, and therefore more impartial judges of the matter, and represented it to them, that the offenders might be convinced, and reformed; if not for fear of God, or love of their brethren, yet at least for the public shame and the cries of the poor. Ezra, and Nehemiah were both good and useful men; but of how different tempers? Ezra was a man of a mild tender spirit, and when told of the sin of the rulers, rent his clothes and wept: Nehemiah forced them to reform, being of a warm and eager spirit. So God's work may be done, and yet different methods taken in doing it; which is a good reason why we should not arraign the management of others, nor make our own standard. (ENOT)

Nehemiah's anger moved him to clear thinking. He continued on to decisive action. He called a meeting for all the community leaders. Courageously, he spoke the truth to these men. He reminded them how, in years gone by, the Jews were enslaved by enemy nations. They had redeemed their kinsmen at great cost. He appealed to their logic. They realized their actions did not make sense. For the other nations to enslave the people of God was a great injustice. Now the well-to-do of Jerusalem were guilty of enslaving their own people. The tyranny of debt, hunger, and taxes was overwhelming enough. But the enslavement of their own people was absolutely intolerable. The men sat in silence! They were guilty and knew it. **They kept quiet, because they could find nothing to say** (v. 8). Nehemiah's courage had won the day.

People who are true leaders are willing to become angry over sin. They also become quiet enough to listen and think. When God shows them a plan of action they are willing to work the plan. God still needs leaders today.

The Paragon of Integrity (Neh. 5:9–10)

The shining brilliance of Nehemiah's integrity is thrilling to behold! He strongly appealed to them to do what was right. Nehemiah was peerless in his practice of doing what was right. In the last two paragraphs of this chapter we find some interesting footnotes to this story. The typical practice was for the governor to receive financial help from the citizens of his district, possibly like a head tax. Nehemiah refused to charge this tax because he had seen their depression and poverty. He also explained that he served meals regularly at his own table. It was common for his cooks to prepare food for 150 people a day. Nehemiah had every right to follow the precedent of previous rulers and accept the tax for support of these meals. He could have amassed wealth and land for himself. He chose to act only for the good of the entire community (vv. 14–18). He was a man of absolute integrity.

Nehemiah refused to accept the evil practices in vogue in his day. His nonconformity came from internal determination to do right. His fear of God was the source of his power to be true.

> ## WORDS FROM WESLEY
> ### Nehemiah 5:9
>
> Watch'd by the world's malignant eye,
> Who load us with reproach and shame,
> As servants of the Lord most high,
> As zealous for His glorious name
> We ought in all His paths to move,
> With holy fear, and humble love.
> That wisdom, Lord, on us bestow,
> From every evil to depart,
> To stop the mouth of every foe,
> While upright both in life and heart,
> The proofs of godly fear we give,
> And show them how the Christians live. (PW, vol. 9, 224)

In Nehemiah's day, there were numbers of wishy-washy politicians. These are still around today. Many church leaders and media preachers have let us down. The call for true integrity seems too hard for so many. God still is calling us to be holy. No matter how the masses are living, God wants us to stand for truth and righteousness. Nehemiah's life shined brightly as a paragon of integrity.

The Promise of Restoration (Neh. 5:11–13)

Dead-end debt dogged the people daily, presenting Nehemiah with one of his many challenges. However, in the face of these great difficulties, Nehemiah demonstrated an impeccable pattern of true leadership. People under his care were complacent and careless, so his excellence stood out as a paragon of purity and integrity. He called for renunciation of the unlawful practices of enslaving and exploiting their own countrymen. On the strength of his pure life, they were ready to obey. He was not merely saying, "Do as I say!" His standard of life proclaimed loudly, "Do as I do! Follow in my steps and you will be following God!"

Fightings Within

People want to follow a leader with integrity. What else could they say? Nehemiah's holy life called out the highest and best in his people.

As Nehemiah dealt with this situation, he showed the people in debt that he identified with them. He was angry with the wrong. He spoke out clearly against sin. His commands were clear and forthright.

He issued a strong order: **Give back to them immediately their fields, vineyards, olive groves and houses, and also the usury you are charging them—the hundredth part of the money, grain, new wine and oil** (v. 11). His leadership was on the line. Nehemiah had set the stage for a win-win response. His was a great victory! Their **promise of restoration** was complete. **We will give it back. . . . And we will not demand anything more from them. We will do as you say** (v. 12). Examine for a moment the extent of their restitution. They returned homes and lands, even the fields and vineyards that had crops on them. They set free any whom they had enslaved and forgave their debts. They burned all mortgages. It was a great day of liberation!

Outstanding leader that he was, Nehemiah carried the agreement one step further. He recognized the promises to restore and forgive could be second guessed. In the future, some might easily say Nehemiah's mandates were too demanding and try to reverse them. So for this covenant, he went public. He called in the priests to witness the men taking the oath. The presence of the priests had strong symbolic significance for the entire community.

After the oath was made, leader Nehemiah carried out one more act of symbolism that would leave an indelible message in their minds. **I also shook out the folds of my robe and said, "In this way may God shake out of his house and possessions every man who does not keep this promise. So may such a man be shaken out and emptied!"** (v. 13).

He must have gathered the front of his robe, lifting it up to form something like a large lap. Then he shook out those folds to give them the picture of how God would shake out and empty any who broke the oath they had made before the priests. When he finished the object lesson, the entire congregation affirmed and applauded his action with a strong **Amen**. Verse 13 has one more important sentence: **And the people did as they had promised.**

WORDS FROM WESLEY
Nehemiah 5:13

My lap—The extreme parts of my garment, which I first folded together, and then shook it and scattered it asunder. This was a form of swearing then in use. (ENOT)

These additional requirements that Nehemiah insisted on—the oath and the shaking out of his robe—suggest some important lessons for the church today. Too often significant decisions and promises are kept private. However, major steps away from sin and toward God are more deeply riveted into the hearts and minds of the members when made public. When the church takes a major stand against ungodliness or when the church takes an unpopular stand for purity and righteousness, every member needs to witness this position. As the church corporately and publicly goes on record to do what is right, we pass on a stirring message to the next generation. The time will come soon when they face similar issues. Let's act in a way that they can follow.

DISCUSSION

Nehemiah helped the Jews rebuild the walls in spite of fierce opposition, but he also helped them sort out an unfortunate financial situation.

1. How did hunger, debt, and taxes threaten the rebuilding of the walls?
2. Why do you agree or disagree that tough economic times threaten the Lord's work?
3. What measures were poorer Jews taking to eat and stay alive?
4. What wrongs were wealthy Jews perpetrating against poorer Jews?
5. Do you think Christian businesspeople should reduce their fees or prices for people who can't afford to pay full price? Why or why not?
6. What advice would you give a newly married couple about debt?
7. Why was Nehemiah's anger justifiable?
8. How did Nehemiah extricate the Jews from their financial crisis?
9. What social injustices, if any, make you rightfully angry? How can you help to relieve or correct a social injustice?

PRAYER

Father, please give us the courage to speak out for the oppressed and needy. Help us to do so with courage, wisdom, and integrity.

8

THE POWER OF THE WORD

Nehemiah 8:1–10, 18; 9:1–3

Understanding God's Word leads to both celebration and confession.

Some congregations stand for the reading of Scripture, but usually the reading lasts only a few minutes. When Nehemiah was governor, the Israelites stood for hours as the book of the law was read. Their riveted attention resulted in a time of national revival.

It has been said that we cannot have revival until we have re-Bible. This study draws your attention to the power of God's Word to convict of sin and inspire obedience to the God of the Word.

COMMENTARY

The seventh month was the most important festival month of the Old Testament year. The first day of the month (the monthly new moon day) was the Feast of Trumpets (compare Num. 29:1–6; Lev. 23:24–25), and 7:73—8:12 is the occasion of the first assembly. On the tenth of the seventh month occurred the Day of Atonement (see Lev. 23:26–32; Num. 29:7–11). No specific reference is made to this in Nehemiah, but the confession of the third assembly in chapters 9–10 fits the spiritual mood and purpose of the Day of Atonement ceremonies. The Feast of Tabernacles then took place on the fifteenth to the twenty-first of the month. The celebration of this festival is described in 8:13–18.

The First Assembly (Neh. 8:1–10)

The current chapter division is somewhat awkward at this point, as the last part of 7:73 seems to be the opening line of this section. During **the seventh month,** specifically **on the first day of the seventh month** (8:2), **the people assembled** (v. 1) in Jerusalem, presumably for the Feast of Trumpets.

The location of the unified assembly (**the people assembled as one man,** v. 1) was **the square before the Water Gate** (v. 1). That city gate, as indicated by its name, was probably next to the Gihon Spring, the water source for the city. The assembly is referred to twice in verses 2–3 as **men, women and others who could understand** (v. 3). This assembly, as well as the day-to-day living out of the covenant obligations, was for the whole family.

The initiative for the reading of the law lay with the people, not the leadership: **They told Ezra . . . to bring out the Book of the Law** (v. 1). Ezra and the Levites were the key leaders at the events of these assemblies. Ezra was designated both as a **scribe** (vv. 1, 4, 9) and **priest** (vv. 2, 9).

WORDS FROM WESLEY
Nehemiah 8:2

First day—This was the feast of trumpets, which is called a sabbath, and on which they were to have an holy convocation. And it was on this day, the altar was set up, after their return from captivity. (ENOT)

The reading of the law by Ezra (**He read it aloud,** v. 3) lasted for some five to six hours (**from daybreak till noon,** v. 3). Verses 3–4 seem to indicate that Ezra was the sole reader during this extended period. The liturgical manner in which the reading was begun displayed the people's respect for the Word of God. Five acts of worship were performed.

1. The people **stood up** at the opening of the book (v. 5). Standing was an act of reverence for the Word of God.

2. Ezra **praised the LORD** (v. 6). Probably such was a brief declaration of praise or the recitation of a psalm, which exalted the character and acts of God.

3. The people **lifted their hands** (v. 6). The lifting up of hands can either be an act of praise or of supplication.

4. The people responded with a verbal response of **"Amen! Amen!"** (v. 6) which literally means "It is firm; it is established." It signifies the listener's assent to what has just been said.

5. The people then **bowed down and worshiped the LORD with their faces to the ground** (v. 6). Kneeling down and bowing with one's face to the ground were primarily acts of obedience.

WORDS FROM WESLEY
Nehemiah 8:7

Understand—As well the words, which being Hebrew, now needed to be translated into the Chaldee or Syriack language, now, the common language of that people, who together with their religion, had also in a great part lost their language; as also the meaning of them: they expounded the mind and will of God in what they read, and applied it to the peoples present condition. (ENOT)

The Levites **instructed the people in the Law** (v. 7), which is repeated in the summary in verse 8 that they were **making it clear and giving the meaning so that the people could understand what was being read**. This instruction in the law was part of their duties and probably involved both explanation and translation. They may have moved among the people as they instructed and answered questions.

While the law was being read, the people's role was one of listening: **All the people listened attentively to the Book of the**

Law (v. 3); **as they listened to the words of the Law** (v. 9). Merely listening to the law was not sufficient; the hearing needed to result in understanding. But the listening and understanding stressed in verses 1–8 then led to behavioral obedience to the law as emphasized in verses 9–12.

The people responded emotionally with **weeping as they listened to the words of the Law** (v. 9). Yet, countering that response is the threefold repetition of the command, **Do not mourn or weep** (v. 9). Given that mourning is deemed an appropriate response in chapters 9–10, why is it not considered the appropriate response here in chapter 8?

There is one primary reason the people are exhorted to be joyful rather than mournful. In verses 9–11—repeated three times with the command not to grieve—is the motivating reason that this occasion was a festival day: **This day is sacred to the LORD your God. Do not mourn or weep** (v. 9); **This day is sacred to our LORD. Do not grieve, for the joy of the LORD is your strength** (v. 10); "Be still, for this is a sacred day. Do not grieve" (v. 11). According to Numbers 10:10, the Feast of Trumpets was to be a festive occasion. Their personal sense of failure to keep the law in the past, which was eliciting the weeping, was not to prevent them from keeping the festival in the joyful manner prescribed by God.

WORDS FROM WESLEY
Nehemiah 8:10

This is the joy my soul desires,
The joy' my Saviour's love inspires,
Which brings the power that sets me free,
Power to renounce whate'er is me;
Power to sell all, and purchase Thee. (PW, vol. 9, 225)

Divinely bestowed joy would become the people's strength. The phrase in verse 10 could be translated "the joy of the LORD is your stronghold," that is, the place or means of protection and safety. The focus of festival celebrations was on the divine acts of deliverance and provision for God's people. Thus the festivals were occasions to focus on the mercy and love of God toward His people rather than on the people's lack of faithfulness.

The command to **send some to those who have nothing prepared** (v. 10) could refer to the poor and the Levites who were unable to prepare anything, or it could also refer to those who, out of laxity or ignorance of the law, had not brought the tithes and offerings they should have. Everyone, whether they had come prepared to do so or not, was able to participate in the celebration.

The Second Assembly (Neh. 8:18)

This gathering on the day after the events of 8:1–12 was unlike the previous assembly in that the first one included all the people, while this one involved only "the heads of all the families, along with the priests and the Levites" (v. 13). This gathering was a consequence of the previous day's proceedings, with the purpose of giving attention to some specific words of the law. The secular leaders were now gathering to determine how the community should observe the upcoming festival.

The Feast of Tabernacles celebrated both the agricultural event of the ingathering of the harvest at the end of the season, as well as the historical event of God's provision during the wilderness period in which the people lived in booths, or tabernacles.

As stipulated twice in Deuteronomy 16:13–15, the celebration of the Feast of Tabernacles was to be a joyous occasion. The Nehemiah narrative notes that the people were obedient even in the spirit in which the celebration was kept (Neh. 8:17).

Leviticus 23:36, 39 and Numbers 29:35 specify that the eighth day was to also incorporate an assembly of the people.

The people's act of obedience to that command is recounted in Nehemiah 8:18: **and on the eighth day . . . there was an assembly.**

In verse 18, during each of the seven days of the feast, the law was read aloud by Ezra to the whole congregation. Although these events in Nehemiah are not specifically stated as occurring during a sabbatical year, it seems that the reading of the law is itself to be understood as an act of obedience in compliance with Deuteronomy 31:10–13, which stipulates that the law was to be read during the Feast of Tabernacles every seventh year.

The Third Assembly (Neh. 9:1–3)

On the twenty-fourth day of the same month (v. 1), just two days following the eighth-day assembly that concluded the Feast of Tabernacles (8:18), **the Israelites** once again **gathered together** (9:1). Unlike the previous two narrated events, which involved the joyous celebration of the festivals (8:12, 17), this assembly was characterized by outward displays of humility and extreme sorrow: **fasting and wearing sackcloth and having dust on their heads** (9:1).

WORDS FROM WESLEY
Nehemiah 9:1

Now—The next day but one after the feast of tabernacles, which begun on the fourteenth day, and ended on the twenty-second, for their consciences having been fully awakened and their hearts filled with grief for their sins, which they were not allowed to express in that time of public joy; now they resume their former thoughts, and recalling their sins to mind, set apart a day for solemn fasting and humiliation. (ENOT)

Also in preparation for this solemn assembly, **Those of Israelite descent had separated themselves from all foreigners**

(v. 2). This refers to the ritual act of segregating out only those of Jewish descent to join this assembly. In other festival gatherings and Sabbaths, the non-Israelite permanent residents (aliens) were permitted and even expected to participate (see Deut. 16:14). Yet this occasion was not a prescribed assembly and was dealing specifically with the sins the Israelites had committed.

Since the laypersons of verse 2 were probably not involved in the reading of the law, in verse 3 the subject, **They**, probably also anticipates the mention of the Levites in verse 4. Thus, **they** incorporates both the lay Israelites who did the **confession and ... worshiping the Lord their God**, as well as the Levites who **read from the Book of the Law of the Lord their God** (v. 3). And both of those groups **stood where they were** (v. 3), while the Levites were "standing on the stairs" (v. 4).

Given the context of confession, in verse 3 their act of **worshiping the Lord their God** probably refers to the physical act of prostrating themselves to the ground. Their bowing is specifically an act of sorrowful humility and petition.

The assembly involved the two primary actions of reading from the book of the law and confessing their sins. Each of these was done for **a quarter of the day** (v. 3), that is, three hours each.

All three of these assemblies involved the reading of the law and the people's responses. The first two reflect a response of careful obedience to the law, characterized by joy. The third assembly involved another appropriate response—that of weeping and confession of sin.

DISCUSSION

Strong walls were important to the security of Jerusalem, but strong faith was essential to every aspect of the Jews' lives. Ears and hearts that were open to God's Word would open a bright future to the nation.

1. Where did the Jews assemble "as one man," and why did they gather together?

2. How long did Ezra read the book of the law to the people? How long do you think Christians today would be willing to stand for the reading of God's Word? Explain your answer.

3. According Nehemiah 8:3, how well did the people listen as Ezra read the book of the law?

4. How did the listeners express their approval of what they heard? How might worshipers today show they approve what they hear from God's Word?

5. How can a preacher or Sunday school teacher help people understand God's Word?

6. Why did the Jews' leaders exhort them not to grieve but to celebrate?

7. Why should collective worship today lead to celebration and obedience?

8. Do you believe public confession of sins is appropriate? If so, when?

PRAYER

Father, we confess that as Your children, we often stray from Your laws. Show us where we have sinned, forgive us, and lead us back into Your will.

9

THE FOOLISH KING AND THE WISE VIRGIN

Esther 1:2–4, 10–12; 2:1–2, 5–7, 15, 17–18

God can work through any circumstance to care for
His people and accomplish His purposes.

"I just happened to be in the right place at the right time." How often have you heard this statement? A hero may say this after saving a heart-attack victim in a restaurant and learning he was the only person there who knew CPR. Or a passerby might say it after rescuing an elderly woman from her burning house. But happenstance doesn't explain a believer's timely intervention in a desperate situation. It can be explained only as divine providence.

God placed Esther—a devout, young Jewish woman—in Persian royalty and used her to save the Jewish nation. This study will increase your awareness that God has placed you where He can use you in astounding ways if you make yourself available to Him.

COMMENTARY

The book of Esther is the story of how a beautiful Jewish woman became the queen of Persia, the wife of Xerxes. It reveals how she and her cousin Mordecai prevented Haman's plot to exterminate the Jewish people. It tells how Mordecai became second only to the king (Est. 10:3). Finally, the book of Esther explains the origin of the Feast of Purim (9:24–28).

This book is unique in several ways. It relates the story of Jews who did not attempt to keep the Mosaic law and who chose to stay in Persia instead of joining the faithful remnant that returned to Jerusalem under Zerubbabel (Ezra 2). In Esther, there are no references to religious convictions or acts except for fasting (Est.

4:16). Esther is not quoted in the New Testament. Another surprising aspect of this book is that the name of God is not mentioned at all. This fact has led some Jewish and Christian scholars to question its right to a place in the Canon.

But even without God's name on open display, His unseen presence and providential power are obviously demonstrated from the beginning to the end of Esther's story. He saved His people with a series of calculated and humorously ironic coincidences. Although the Lord is not plainly linked with the Jews who stayed in exile, His care for them is undeniable. They were His covenant people, and He protected them from the "ethnic cleansing" intended for them.

The study passage introduces the three main characters of this story: Xerxes, the king of Persia; Esther, who becomes his queen; and Mordecai, her cousin and guardian.

The Banquet Blowout (Est. 1:2–4)

At that time King Xerxes (v. 2). This was probably Xerxes I (486–465 B.C.). He confronted the same problems that had plagued his father, Darius. The Persian Empire was crumbling, primarily because of the tax load. However, unlike his father, Xerxes did not care about retaining the loyalty of his subjects, and he made unfortunate decisions in his military actions. For example, Xerxes infuriated the Egyptian priests by stealing their temple treasures. He burned Athens and forfeited all possible backing from the Greek city-states. He destroyed Babylon's temples and ordered that Marduk's golden statue be melted down. Xerxes's history lines up well with the impulsive and irritable king described in the book of Esther.

Xerxes reigned from his royal throne in the citadel of Susa (v. 2). Susa was the ancient capital of Elam (Gen. 14). The site is in southwestern Iran at the current village of Shush, about 150 miles north of the Persian Gulf. When Cyrus the Great set up the

Persian Empire, he made Susa its capital, and Darius the Great (father of Xerxes) built his dazzling royal palace there. Most of the events in the book of Esther happen in that palace.

In the third year of his reign he gave a banquet for all his nobles and officials (Est. 1:3). An ancient Greek historian named Herodotus reported that Xerxes assembled his key leaders to plan a war with Greece. This may very well be the same event, since the **military leaders of Persia and Media, the princes, and the nobles of the provinces were present** (v. 3).

This event was lavish and long. **For a full 180 days he displayed the vast wealth of his kingdom and the splendor and glory of his majesty** (v. 4). This probably did not last nonstop for 180 days. It's more likely that this was the time required to display his treasures and wealth. Different military leaders, princes, and nobles almost certainly came at different times throughout this period, since the empire stretched from India in the east to the upper Nile River valley in the west.

WORDS FROM WESLEY

Esther 1:4

Many days—Making every day a magnificent feast, either for all his princes, or for some of them, who might come to the feast successively, as the king ordered them to do. The Persian feasts are much celebrated in authors, for their length and luxury. (ENOT)

After satisfying his vanity by showing his wealth and majesty to his subjects, Xerxes held a weeklong banquet "for all the people from the least to the greatest, who were in the citadel of Susa" in his royal gardens (1:5–8). His wife at that time was Queen Vashti ("the best"). She held a banquet for the women "in the royal palace of King Xerxes" at the same time (1:9). Royal Persian feasts were well-known for their luxury and lavishness.

Esther describes the Persian custom of eating while reclining on beds or couches. In this case, the couches were made of gold and silver (1:6). This and other statements about the customs of the Persian court support the idea that this book was written by an eyewitness. At the least it must be based on the records of one who was there.

The Royal Blowup (Est. 1:10–12)

On the seventh and last **day** of the banquet, **King Xerxes was in high spirits from wine** (v. 10). He was most certainly drunk and even more impulsive than usual. **He commanded the seven eunuchs who served him ... to bring before him Queen Vashti, wearing her royal crown, in order to display her beauty to the people and nobles, for she was lovely to look at** (vv. 10–11). Since Persian modesty required women to wear veils in public, it looks as if Xerxes was asking her to disgrace herself to comply with his drunken urge. Some commentators have suggested the possibility that what the king ultimately wanted was for Vashti to exhibit her naked body to his guests because she was so beautiful. This would have put her on the same level as the wealth and possessions displayed during the 180 days. **But when the attendants delivered the king's command, Queen Vashti refused to come** (v. 12). This woman refused to be viewed as a mere object and possession. She risked her life to maintain her dignity.

WORDS FROM WESLEY
Esther 1:12

Refused—Being favoured in this refusal by the law of Persia, which was to keep mens wives, and especially queens, from the view of other men. (ENOT)

Then the king became furious and burned with anger (v. 12). This was to be expected. Xerxes tended to make rash and angry decisions, and he was drunk. As a king, his authority was absolute. No one could say no to a king without expecting to be executed.

In an effort to protect their kings from assassination, the Persians limited the number of persons who could meet with them face-to-face. The Greek historian Herodotus and Ezra 7:14 indicate that these special counselors were limited to seven men. At the time of the banquet, they were "Carshena, Shethar, Admatha, Tarshish, Meres, Marsena and Memucan, the seven nobles of Persia and Media who had special access to the king and were highest in the kingdom" (1:14). These advisors suggested through Memucan that the king make an irreversible decree banishing Vashti and giving her royal position to another. The goal was to make "all the women . . . respect their husbands, from the least to the greatest" (1:20). A "royal decree . . . written in the laws of Persia and Media, [could not] be repealed" (1:19; Dan. 6). King Xerxes approved of this plan, so he utilized the empire's fine postal service to spread the news. "He sent dispatches to all parts of the kingdom, to each province in its own script and to each people in its own language, proclaiming in each people's tongue that every man should be ruler over his own household" (1:22).

The Royal Roundup (Est. 2:1–2)

About three years later (2:16), **the anger of King Xerxes had subsided** (v. 1). Since it seems that the banquet described in chapter 1 was for planning his invasion of Greece, Xerxes was probably at war for the intervening years. But the Greeks defeated him, and he returned to a palace without a queen to console him. In this depressed and lonely frame of mind, **Xerxes . . . remembered Vashti and what she had done and what he had decreed about her** (v. 1). So **the king's personal attendants**

(v. 2) made a proposal—perhaps to keep the king from punishing them for their advice about Vashti. They said, **"Let a search be made for beautiful young virgins for the king"** (v. 2). They went on to add, "Let the king appoint commissioners in every province of his realm to bring all these beautiful girls into the harem at the citadel of Susa. Let them be placed under the care of Hegai, the king's eunuch, who is in charge of the women; and let beauty treatments be given to them. Then let the girl who pleases the king be queen instead of Vashti" (2:3–4). This recommendation fascinated Xerxes, so he went along with it.

The Heroes (Est. 2:5–7)

Now there was in the citadel of Susa a Jew of the tribe of Benjamin, named Mordecai (v. 5). He was the **son of Jair, the son of Shimei, the son of Kish** (father of Israel's first king, Saul). Over one hundred years before, Mordecai's family **had been carried into exile from Jerusalem by Nebuchadnezzar king of Babylon, among those taken captive with Jehoiachin king of Judah** (v. 6). This was the exile prophesied by Isaiah (Isa. 39) and Jeremiah (Jer. 20:1–6; 27:16–22; 29:1–23) and a pivotal time for the Jewish people. The prophet Daniel would have been a contemporary of Mordecai's ancestors.

WORDS FROM WESLEY
Esther 2:5

Esther—Hadassah was her Hebrew name before her marriage; and she was called Esther by the king after it. (ENOT)

Mordecai had a younger **cousin named Hadassah** (Est. 2:7, which means "myrtle"). He had raised her like his own daughter **because she had neither father nor mother**. They had died.

This girl, who was also known as Esther (which means "star"), **was lovely in form and features** (v. 7). So, she was "taken to the king's palace and entrusted to Hegai, who had charge of the harem" (2:8). She soon became Hegai's favorite, and he provided her with special treatments as well as "the best place in the harem" (2:9).

Mordecai had forbidden Esther from revealing her ethnic origin, so she did not tell anyone she was a Jew (2:10, 20). Even though Mordecai could not see Esther face-to-face, he would stand outside the courtyard of the harem to ask others about her. They were able to exchange messages in the same way (2:11, 20).

Unforgettable Girl (Est. 2:15, 17–18)

Each of these beautiful virgins was prepared to meet the king after undergoing a year of beauty treatments and purification baths. They used the oil of myrrh for six months and perfumes and cosmetics for the final six months. Each young woman had one night to impress the king. She could take anything with her that she wanted, everything else was left behind. After spending the night in the king's bed, she would be sent "to another part of the harem to the care of Shaashgaz, the king's eunuch who was in charge of the concubines" (2:14). The concubines were women who had slept with the king and so could not be with any other man. On top of that, a concubine would never see the king again unless he called for her by name (2:14). They lived a lonely life in a luxurious prison.

When the turn came for Esther ... to go to the king, she asked for nothing other than what Hegai ... suggested (v. 15). No one knew what Xerxes liked more than Hegai. It appears Esther realized this and chose to match up to those desires as she went in to the king. **Esther ... won his favor and approval more than any of the other virgins** (v. 17). It looks as if she was beautiful in appearance and temperament.

> **WORDS FROM WESLEY**
> *Esther 2:13*
>
> *Desired*—For ornament, or by way of attendance. And it should be observed, that every one whom the king took to his bed, was his wife of a lower rank, as Hagar was Abraham's, so that it would have been no sin or dishonour to Esther, though she had not been made queen. (ENOT)

"She was taken to King Xerxes in the royal residence in the tenth month, the month of Tebeth, in the seventh year of his reign" (2:16). This may have been in December of 479 B.C. or in January of 478 B.C. Either way, it began her reign as queen of Persia because **the king was attracted to Esther more than to any of the other women** (v. 17). Something about her set Esther apart. As a result, Xerxes **set a royal crown on her head and made her queen instead of Vashti** (v. 17).

Esther 1:2–4, 10–12; 2:1–2, 5–7, 15, 17–18

DISCUSSION

King Xerxes had power, fame, servants, and wealth, but as you read the opening chapters you will discover he lacked wisdom.

1. How did Xerxes flaunt his wealth and power? What other people in the Bible did this?

2. Why did Xerxes order his servants to bring Queen Vashti into the banquet hall?

3. Why did Vashti's conduct worry the King's consultants?

4. Read Esther 1:19–22. Would you characterize Xerxes as a male chauvinist? Why or why not?

5. Why do you think the king was so attracted to Esther? Do you see the hand of God in her appointment to be queen? Why or why not?

PRAYER

Father, as we faithfully follow You, help us to trust that You are leading, even when the path You lead us on doesn't make sense to us.

10

THE VARIED FACES OF EVIL

Esther 2:19–23; 3:1–6, 8–11

God's plan is never thwarted by evil actions.

God's people have never been popular. Through the centuries, devout men and women have been hunted and even killed for their faith (Heb. 11:33–38). Nero tied Christians to stakes in his garden and set them ablaze. The blood of martyrs flowed freely in the Middle Ages, and in some countries today, our fellow believers are severely persecuted for their faith. In the book of Esther, we read about Mordecai, a devout Jew, who refused to bow down and honor evil Haman. His devotion to God and defiance of Haman brought Haman's wrath down on his head, but God would have the last word.

You expect opposition to your faith, but this study will buoy your courage to stand for God.

COMMENTARY

The book of Esther tells the story of how a beautiful Jewish woman became the queen of Persia, the wife of Xerxes I. It reveals how Queen Esther and her cousin-guardian, Mordecai, thwarted the extermination of the entire Jewish population that was planned by Haman. It explains how Mordecai eventually became second only to King Xerxes (Est. 10:3). Ultimately, the book of Esther explains the origin of the Feast of Purim (9:24–28), which is still celebrated by God's chosen people.

The verses for this study expose Mordecai's loyalty to the king. They also introduce the fourth main character and the villain of this story—Haman—whom Xerxes makes second in command over the whole empire.

A Plot Exposed (Est. 2:19–23)

Later **the virgins were assembled a second time** (v. 19), most likely to continue expanding the king's harem. **Mordecai was sitting at the king's gate** (v. 19). The city gates were the places of business and legal transactions. That Mordecai was sitting there indicates he held an important position in the empire's civil service. Archeological evidence reveals that a minister in the court of Susa had a name similar to Mordecai. He may have been the governor of Babylon at one time. Some scholars believe this evidence refers to the Mordecai of Esther.

WORDS FROM WESLEY
Esther 2:19

Sat—By office, as one of the king's guards or ministers; being advanced to this place by Esther's favour. (ENOT)

Although Mordecai was known at the king's gate, **Esther had kept secret her family background and nationality just as Mordecai had told her to do** (v. 20). We don't know why Mordecai instructed Esther to keep her ethnic origin a secret. Esther may not have asked the reason, because **she continued to follow Mordecai's instructions as she had done when he was bringing her up** (v. 20). Queen Esther still gave Mordecai the respect and obedience she had developed as a child in his home.

One day while **Mordecai was sitting at the king's gate, Bigthana and Teresh, two of the king's officers who guarded the doorway, became angry and conspired to assassinate**

King Xerxes (v. 21). These kinds of hostile coups were not unusual. **But Mordecai found out about the plot and** sent a message to **Queen Esther, who in turn reported it to the king** (v. 22). Esther made sure to give the **credit** for saving the king's life **to Mordecai. And when the report was investigated and found to be true, the two officials were hanged on a gallows** (vv. 22–23). The NIV text notes point out that they probably were "impaled on a pole." Impalement was the Persian means of hanging someone. Darius I, Xerxes's father, impaled three thousand Babylonians when he crushed their rebellion. **All this was recorded in the book of the annals in the presence of the king** (v. 23). The Persians kept meticulous records, a detail that comes into play throughout this story.

The Villain Arrives (Est. 3:1–6)

After these events, King Xerxes honored Haman son of Hammedatha, the Agagite (v. 1). Based on Esther 2:16–17 and 3:7, four years passed between Esther's coronation and Haman's promotion. Haman was an Agagite, a descendent of Agag the king of the Amalekites. Israel's first king, Saul, lost the throne because he disobeyed God's command to destroy the Amalekites completely. Xerxes elevated Haman and gave **him a seat of honor higher than that of all the other nobles. All the royal officials at the king's gate** where Mordecai worked **knelt down and paid honor to Haman** (vv. 1–2). Note that Haman did not instigate this admiration. **The king had commanded this concerning him** (v. 2).

Xerxes demanded that the other administrators in his court bow in respect to Haman, **but Mordecai would not kneel down or pay him honor. Then the royal officials at the king's gate asked Mordecai, "Why do you disobey the king's command?"** (vv. 2–3). That kind of behavior could have proven deadly. Perhaps Mordecai was refusing to worship a mere man, but neither he nor Esther seemed to follow the Mosaic law. It is most likely that Mordecai would not kneel down to an Amalekite, an enemy of the Jewish people. **Day after day his coworkers spoke to him but** Mordecai **refused to comply** (v. 4). Finally they gave up and **told Haman about it to see whether Mordecai's behavior would be tolerated** (v. 4). It appears that the only reason Mordecai would give for his disobedience was to say **he was a Jew** (v. 4). This gives further support to the idea that his motivation was more ethnic pride than religious conviction.

WORDS FROM WESLEY
Esther 3:2

Probably the worship required was not only civil, but Divine: which as the kings of Persia arrogated to themselves, so they did sometimes impart this honour to some of their chief favourites, that they should be adored in like manner. And that it was so here, seems more than probable, because it was superfluous, to give an express command to all the king's servants, to pay a civil respect to so great a prince, which of course they used, and therefore a Divine honour must be here intended. And that a Jew should deny this honour, is not strange, seeing the wise Grecians did positively refuse to give this honour to the kings of Persia themselves, even when they were to make their addresses to them: and one Timocrates was put to death by the Athenians for worshiping Darius in that manner. (ENOT)

When Haman saw that Mordecai would not kneel down or pay him honor, he was enraged (v. 5). It's hard to believe Haman had never noticed Mordecai standing while everyone else knelt. **Yet** once he was informed **who Mordecai's people were, he scorned the idea of killing only Mordecai** (v. 6). Punishing one person for not bowing in his presence would not satisfy Haman's ethnic hatred. **Instead Haman looked for a way to destroy all Mordecai's people, the Jews, throughout**

the whole kingdom of Xerxes (v. 6). Notice how the author built the intensity in this sentence: First with Mordecai's people (personal), then extending the threat to the Jews (racial), and finally to the whole kingdom of Xerxes (geographical).

Esther 3:7 gives some vital bits of information: "In the twelfth year of King Xerxes, in the first month, the month of Nisan, they cast the pur (that is, the lot) in the presence of Haman to select a day and month. And the lot fell on the twelfth month, the month of Adar." In the month the Jews celebrated the Feast of Passover (Ex. 12), Haman cast lots to determine when it would be best to destroy them. The plural of *pur* is *purim* and would become the ironic name of the feast celebrating the Jews' rescue from Haman. The result of casting the lot indicated a date for killing the Jews that was nearly a year away. That gave enough time for a rescue to be mounted.

WORDS FROM WESLEY
Esther 3:6

Scorn—He thought that vengeance was unsuitable to his quality. *Destroy*—Which he attempted, from that implacable hatred which, as an Amalekite, he had against them; from his rage against Mordecai; and from Mordecai's reason of this contempt, because he was a Jew, which as he truly judged, extended itself to all the Jews, and would equally engage them all in the same neglect. And doubtless Haman included those who were returned to their own land: for that was now a province of his kingdom. (ENOT)

Casting lots was frequently used to make important decisions. The Jewish priests used it to determine which goat would be sacrificed and which one would be released in the wilderness (Lev. 16:6–10). The writer of Proverbs said, "The lot is cast into the lap, but its every decision is from the LORD" (Prov. 16:33). The last time it was used by God's people was when the disciples used it to choose a replacement for Judas Iscariot (Acts 1:15–26). From then on, decisions were made with praying and fasting (13:1–3; 14:23).

The Villain Lies (Est. 3:8–11)

After determining his best date for attacking the Jews, Haman lied to King Xerxes. But like all believable falsehoods, this one contained some truth. **Haman said to King Xerxes, "There is a certain people dispersed and scattered among the peoples in all the provinces of your kingdom whose customs are different from those of all other people"** (v. 8). This much is true. The Jewish people had been dispersed and scattered throughout the Middle East because of God's judgment. Their customs were different from those of others, but that is true of every ethnic group. Persians had Persian customs, Babylonians had their own customs, and so on.

In spite of these truths, Haman added an exaggeration that made his whole statement a manipulative lie. He told the king, these people **do not obey the king's laws; it is not in the king's best interest to tolerate them** (v. 8). The truth was that only one person refused to obey one of the king's decrees. Mordecai would not bow down to Haman.

Haman suggested a way to solve his manufactured problem. **"If it pleases the king, let a decree be issued to destroy them"** (v. 9). Haman used one of Xerxes's constant problems to his own evil advantage. Xerxes had inherited from his father an empire that was ready to fall apart at the seams. Here Haman seemed to present the king with a simple way to unify his kingdom: Exterminate an entire group of troublemakers, and perhaps the others will submit to Persian rule quietly. But Haman went further and offered a monetary incentive as well: **"I will put ten thousand talents of silver into the royal treasury for the men who carry out this business"** (v. 9). The royal treasury was probably short on funds because of the war with Greece. Ten thousand talents of silver is equivalent to over 350 tons of the precious metal. Haman must have expected to confiscate the Jews' property for the king.

So the king took his signet ring from his finger and gave it to Haman son of Hammedatha, the Agagite, the enemy of the Jews (v. 10). Xerxes was an impulsive man. In one quick motion, he turned his power over to Haman. The signet ring was his tool for signing his decrees. It was the emblem of Xerxes's royal authority. By giving it to Haman, the king expressed his complete trust in Haman to do what was best for the kingdom. Xerxes also gave Haman his verbal blessing by saying, **"Keep the money ... and do with the people as you please"** (v. 11). So Haman became **the enemy** or persecutor **of the Jews** (v. 10). Letters carrying the decree to destroy the Jews were sent out to "each province and in the language of each people ... to the king's satraps, the governors of the various provinces and the nobles of the various peoples" (3:12). The order "to destroy, kill and annihilate all the Jews—young and old, women and little children—on ... the thirteenth day of the twelfth month ... and to plunder their goods" was a decree that could not be repealed or changed (3:13). So Xerxes and Haman celebrated their victory with alcoholic beverages, but everyone else in the city was confused. The edict did not make sense to them. It may have worried those who were not Persians, causing them to wonder if their people could be singled out for annihilation as well.

Esther 2:19–23; 3:1–6, 8–11

DISCUSSION

Villains who scheme to try to destroy God's people and disrupt His plan learn the hard way that no one wins a battle against God. Watch how this truth plays out in the book of Esther.

1. How did Mordecai save Xerxes's life?

2. How was Mordecai credited with preventing the assassination attempt?

3. If you were to list Haman's evil characteristics, which one would top the list? Why?

4. How did Haman use Mordecai's refusal to bow down to him as an opportunity to vent his anti-Semitism?

5. How did the king and Haman celebrate their binding edict to annihilate the Jews?

6. Why is racial prejudice, including anti-Semitism, offensive to God?

7. How do you explain the survival of the Jewish people through centuries of persecution?

PRAYER

Father, help us remember that even when our enemies seem to be winning the battle, in the end, You will win the war.

11

GODLY CHARACTER MEETS CHALLENGES WITH GODLINESS

Esther 4:1, 4; 4:12—5:9

God sometimes asks us to do more than we think we can, but He always provides a way.

Queen for a Day was a popular TV show in the 1950s. It crowned a winning housewife "queen for a day" and lavished her with many valuable prizes. In a sense, Esther was queen for a day—the day God had appointed for her to gain the king's favor and start the wheels in motion to save her people, the Jews, from genocide.

As a result of this study, you will approach each day not just as another day, but as a day of opportunity to serve God as He chooses.

COMMENTARY

God is never mentioned in the book of Esther, but His invisible presence and power are easily perceived. God saved His covenant people with a series of twists and turns. Although the Lord is not linked with the Jews who stayed in Persia, His care for them is undeniable. They were His people, and He protected them from the "ethnic cleansing" intended for them.

In chapter 1, Queen Vashti was expelled for refusing King Xerxes's drunken request. In chapter 2, a beautiful, young, Jewish girl named Esther captured the king's heart and became the new queen. Then her cousin-guardian Mordecai prevented an assassination planned against King Xerxes. In chapter 3, Haman, a descendant of Israel's ancient enemy the Amalekites, was promoted above all Persia's princes. Then he misled the king into decreeing the death of all Jews. The text for this study reveals how Mordecai and Esther respond to the threat against them.

Mordecai and His People Grieve (Est. 4:1, 4)

When Mordecai learned of all that had been done, he tore his clothes, put on sackcloth and ashes, and went out into the city, wailing loudly and bitterly (v. 1). Each one of these acts was an expression of grief and distress. Combining all three reveals the depth of Mordecai's despair after hearing the fatal decree. He went out into the city because the palace was intended to shelter the king from the painful realities of life. Grieving persons were not allowed to enter.

WORDS FROM WESLEY

Esther 4:1

Cry—To express his deep sense of the mischief coming upon his people. It was bravely done, thus publicly to espouse a just cause though it seemed to be a desperate one. (ENOT)

That's the reason Mordecai "went only as far as the king's gate, because no one clothed in sackcloth was allowed to enter" the palace (4:2). Mordecai was not the only person to express his distress openly. "In every province to which the edict and order of the king came, there was great mourning among the Jews, with fasting, weeping and wailing. Many lay in sackcloth and ashes" (4:3).

Although Mordecai could not enter the palace, those who knew his relationship to Esther noticed his loud demonstrations of sorrow. Some of them must have been **Esther's maids and eunuchs**, because they **came and told her about Mordecai**

(v. 4). When Esther heard about her cousin's grief, **she was in great distress. She sent clothes for him to put on instead of his sackcloth, but he would not accept them** (v. 4). When Mordecai refused to be comforted, Esther sent one of the eunuchs assigned to her to find out what was troubling him and why.

The eunuch found "Mordecai in the open square of the city in front of the king's gate" (v. 6). He told the eunuch everything about the decree, "including the exact amount of money Haman had promised to pay into the royal treasury for the destruction of the Jews" (v. 7). The extent of Mordecai's knowledge of Haman's conversation with the king indicates how high a position he held in the court. Mordecai also sent a copy of the order for the genocide to Esther. He asked the eunuch to explain it to Esther and encourage her to beg King Xerxes for mercy. Someone needed to plead with him for the Jewish people (v. 8).

So the eunuch went back to Esther and told her what Mordecai had said. Since Mordecai's open mourning prevented him from entering the palace and since she was confined to the harem quarters, Esther told her eunuch to remind Mordecai that access to the king was limited. She said, "All the king's officials and the people of the royal provinces know that for any man or woman who approaches the king in the inner court without being summoned the king has but one law: that he be put to death. The only exception to this is for the king to extend the gold scepter to him and spare his life. But thirty days have passed since I was called to go to the king" (v. 11). The Greek historian Herodotus reports this tradition as well. So Esther was reluctant to approach the king, especially since he had not spoken to her for a month.

Perhaps You're Queen for This Time (Est. 4:12–17)

Mordecai's response to Queen Esther's reluctance to approach the king uninvited is a key to understanding the message of this book. Mordecai **sent back this answer: "Do not think that because you are in the king's house you alone of all the Jews will escape. For if you remain silent at this time, relief and deliverance for the Jews will arise from another place, but you and your father's family will perish. And who knows but that you have come to royal position for such a time as this?"** (vv. 13–14).

> ### WORDS FROM WESLEY
> *Esther 4:13*
>
> Ye that in royal mansions live,
> And Christ into your hearts receive,
> Think not to serve your Saviour's cause,
> Yet 'scape the scandal of His cross:
> In Caesar's house, to save your fame,
> Ye must deny your Master's name,
> Or bear, if Christ ye dare confess,
> The mark of Jesu's witnesses. (PW, vol. 9, 228)

Mordecai was certain of several things. First, Haman would make sure Mordecai would be one of the first Jews to die. Second, Esther's life was already in danger. She would perish with her family if she said nothing. The safest thing she could do would be to approach the king and hope he would pardon her interruption. Third, the Jews would be delivered by some other means. Mordecai did not say God would save His people, but he certainly implied it. Finally, Mordecai suggested that Esther's rise to become queen of Persia was in preparation for this life-and-death crisis.

Esther responded by asking Mordecai and all the Jews of Susa to fast for her (v. 16). This is as close to mentioning prayer as the book of Esther comes. As a result, Mordecai did exactly what she said to do.

> ### WORDS FROM WESLEY
> #### Esther 4:14
> *From another place*—This was the language of strong faith, against hope believing in hope. *Who knoweth*—It is probable God hath raised thee to this honour for this very season. We should every one of us consider, for what end God has put us in the place where we are? And when an opportunity offers of serving God and our generation, we must take care not to let it slip. (ENOT)

Esther Visits the King (Est. 5:1–9)

On the third day of the fast, **Esther put on her royal robes** (v. 1) in order to look her best for the king. Then Esther **stood in the inner court of the palace** and **in front of the king's hall**, where she could be seen easily. **The king was sitting on his royal throne in the hall, facing the entrance. When he saw Queen Esther standing in the court, he was pleased with her and held out to her the gold scepter that was in his hand** (vv. 1–2). He spared her life. **So Esther approached and touched the tip of the scepter** (v. 2) and received his pardon for interrupting the king's business.

The king (v. 3) must have known something important was on Esther's mind since she had risked her life to approach him. He **asked, "What is it, Queen Esther? What is your request? Even up to half the kingdom, it will be given you"** (v. 3). This offer was probably a figure of speech meant to imply anything within reason. Esther's answer seems surprising, but she may have been preparing the king to hear a very serious request. So she invited Xerxes and Haman **to a banquet** she had **prepared for** them (v. 4).

"Bring Haman at once," the king said, "so that we may do what Esther asks" (v. 5). Kings and queens seldom ate together, and to invite a man to the meal who was not related to either of them would have been very unusual. Later, Haman bragged to his friends and family that he was "the only person Queen Esther invited to accompany the king to the banquet she gave" (5:12).

So the king and Haman went to the banquet Esther had prepared. As they were drinking wine, the king again asked Esther, "Now what is your petition? It will be given you. And what is your request? Even up to half the kingdom, it will be granted" (vv. 5–6). Xerxes repeated his willingness to grant Esther nearly anything she asked.

Esther replied, "My petition and my request is this: If the king regards me with favor and if it pleases the king to grant my petition and fulfill my request, let the king and Haman come tomorrow to the banquet I will prepare for them. Then I will answer the king's question" (vv. 7–8). In other words, Esther told the king she wanted to wait one more day before giving him the answer about what she really wanted. The reason for her delay may not have been obvious to Xerxes, but God wanted a night to work in the king's heart and mind (see 6:1–3).

WORDS FROM WESLEY
Esther 5:8

Tomorrow—I will acquaint thee with my humble request. She did not present her petition at this time, but delayed it 'till the next meeting; either because she was a little daunted with the king's presence, or, because she would farther engage the king's affection to her, and would also intimate to him that her petition was of a more than ordinary nature: but principally by direction of Divine providence, which took away her courage of utterance for this time, that she might have a better opportunity for it the next time, by that great accident which happened before it. (ENOT)

Haman went out that day happy and in high spirits (5:9). He had been honored by the king and promoted over all the princes and nobles. He had been a unique guest at an unusual banquet given by the queen for the king. He must have thought, "Life can't get better than this." **But when he saw Mordecai at the king's gate and observed that he neither rose nor showed fear in his presence, he was filled with rage against Mordecai** (v. 9). One lone man refusing to fear him infuriated Haman. He was no longer satisfied with being honored. He wanted people to fear him too.

Haman went home without punishing Mordecai, which should have been well within his authority. When he arrived, he attempted to soothe his hurt feelings by boasting to his friends and wife. Haman bragged "to them about his vast wealth, his many sons, and all the ways the king had honored him and how he had elevated him above the other nobles and officials" (v. 11). All of these things were considered marks of real success and genuine manhood. He even bragged about eating with King Xerxes and Queen Esther. "And she has invited me along with the king [to eat with her again] tomorrow. But all this gives me no satisfaction as long as I see that Jew Mordecai sitting at the king's gate" (vv. 12–13). Even though Haman possessed enormous treasures, glory, and honor, and was the king's premier favorite, he was miserable because he could not have the honor of the very man he despised and wanted to kill.

In order to cheer up their benefactor, Haman's wife and friends suggested that he "have a gallows built, seventy-five feet high" (v. 14). Then he could ask the king first thing in the morning to have Mordecai hanged on it, or the Persians' version which involved impaling the victim on a sharp pole and leaving him there to die. That way Haman could really enjoy the banquet with the king and queen. "This suggestion delighted Haman, and he had the gallows built" (v. 14).

DISCUSSION

This study sets the stage for a great victory for the Jews. Observe how Esther, a young Jewish woman, had come to the kingdom for a crucial moment in history.

1. How did Mordecai and the Jews respond to Xerxes and Haman's death decree?
2. How do you find hope in desperate circumstances?
3. What risk would Esther be taking if she approached King Xerxes uninvited? What persuaded her to take the risk?
4. Do you sense that God has placed you in a certain job or neighborhood for a specific purpose? If so, are you willing to fulfill that purpose even if risk is involved?
5. What support did Mordecai pledge on Esther's behalf?
6. How have prayers of friends and loved ones encouraged you in the past?
7. When Esther received the king's permission to approach him with a request, what plan did she set in motion?
8. What was Haman's burning desire?

PRAYER

Father, guide us as we seek to follow Your will. Grant us wisdom in our planning and in the decisions we make along the way.

12

GOD HONORS RIGHTEOUSNESS AND FAITHFULNESS

Esther 6:1–10; 7:1–10; 10:3

God honors our efforts to cooperate with His plans for good.

Circumstances looked bleak for Esther. Mordecai wore a target on his back; Haman had him in his sights; the Jews were singled out for annihilation; and the edict to destroy them was set in stone. But nothing panics God. He disturbed the king of Persia's sleep and caused him to remember Mordecai and reward him. God also used Esther in a surprising way to seal Haman's doom.

Through this study, you will learn to trust God in all of life's circumstances, regardless how threatening they seem.

COMMENTARY

To recap, in Esther 1, King Xerxes held a lavish celebration in his royal capital of Susa. On the seventh day, he called for Queen Vashti to come and expose her beauty to his guests. When she refused, the king asked his advisors what could be done. They suggested an irrevocable decree that would depose Vashti and declare that "every man should be ruler over his own household" (1:22). This pleased the king, and so male domination of women became the legal norm throughout the empire.

Chapter 2 tells us that three years later, possibly after a humiliating defeat, Xerxes began to long for Vashti. So his advisors suggested a beauty contest to seek a new queen to take her place. The king approved of their plans, and young virgin women were rounded up from around the empire.

Mordecai, a Jew from the tribe of Benjamin, had raised his orphaned niece, Esther, after her parents died. They were cousins, although Mordecai must have been old enough to be her father. Esther was one of the beautiful young women taken into the king's harem.

When Esther's turn came to spend the night with King Xerxes, he fell in love with her and made her his new queen. However, in all the time she lived in the harem, Esther never revealed to anyone in the palace that she was a Jew.

In chapter 3, Haman, a descendant of Israel's ancient enemy the Amalekites, was promoted above all Persia's princes. Then he misled the king into decreeing the death of all Jews. Casting lots set the date for the massacre.

When Mordecai heard the proclamation, he went into mourning and pleaded with Esther to intercede for her people. Esther agreed to his request, knowing that anyone entering the throne room without an invitation would be executed unless the king pardoned him or her. Xerxes extended his scepter to Esther and received her with a promise to grant any petition she might have. She invited the king and Haman to a private banquet. There the king repeated his promise to grant her request "up to half of the kingdom." Esther simply invited King Xerxes and Haman to another dinner to be held the next day.

These invitations fueled Haman's pride and anger when Mordecai refused to honor him. At the suggestion of his wife and friends, Haman built a gallows outside his house. He planned to ask for the king's permission to hang Mordecai there. The text for this study reveals how God turned the tables on Haman and saved the Jews.

Paying a Debt of Honor (Est. 6:1–10)

That night (after the banquet hosted by Esther) **the king could not sleep** (v. 1). Just as the king must have tossed and turned in his bed, this verse turns the whole outcome of the book.

Perhaps it was his curiosity about the queen's mysterious request or maybe God gave him a nagging sense of an unpaid debt. Whatever the reason, Xerxes was sleepless, **so he ordered the book of the chronicles, the record of his reign, to be brought in and read to him** (v. 1). As the scribes read to him, **it was found** (at God's unseen direction) **recorded there that Mordecai had exposed Bigthana and Teresh, two of the king's officers who guarded the doorway, who had conspired to assassinate King Xerxes** (v. 2; see 2:21–23).

WORDS FROM WESLEY
Esther 6:1

Sleep—How vain are all the contrivances of foolish man against the wise and omnipotent God, who hath the hearts and hands of kings and all men perfectly at His disposal, and can by such trivial accidents (as they are accounted) change their minds, and produce such terrible effects. *Were read*—His mind being troubled he knew not how, nor why, he chooses this for a diversion, God putting this thought into him, for otherwise he might have diverted himself, as he used to do, with his wives or concubines, or voices and instruments of music, which were far more agreeable to his temper. (ENOT)

Recognizing that Mordecai had shown him great loyalty, Xerxes asked the scribes, **"What honor and recognition has Mordecai received for this?"** (6:3). Their answer must have startled the king because they replied, **"Nothing has been done for him"** (v. 3).

The king responded to this situation with a decisive desire to make things right as soon as possible. He **said, "Who is in the court?"** (v. 4). As a rule, a high-ranking official was assigned to be nearby for the king in case he needed to talk and to seek the official's advice. **Now** (right in God's time) **Haman had just**

entered the outer court of the palace to speak to the king about hanging Mordecai on the gallows he had erected for him (v. 4). The irony here is amazing. Mordecai was on the minds of both the king and Haman. Xerxes was seeking to pay honor to a loyal subject, while Haman was planning to kill a man who would not honor him.

The king's **attendants answered, "Haman is standing in the court"** (v. 5). **"Bring him in," the king ordered** (v. 5). So Haman was ushered in to see the king.

When Haman entered, the king asked him a general question, seeking Haman's advice: **"What should be done for the man the king delights to honor?"** (v. 6). The fact that Xerxes withheld the identity of the man he planned to honor is poetic justice for Haman, who withheld the identity of the people he wished to destroy (3:7–10).

Now Haman thought to himself, "Who is there that the king would rather honor than me?" So he answered the king with his fondest dream, **"For the man the king delights to honor, have them bring a royal robe the king has worn and a horse the king has ridden, one with a royal crest placed on its head. Then let the robe and horse be entrusted to one of the king's most noble princes. Let them robe the man the king delights to honor, and lead him on the horse through the city streets, proclaiming before him, 'This is what is done for the man the king delights to honor!'"** (6:6–9).

In the ancient world, wearing a powerful person's clothes was a sign of high honor and, in this case, of sharing the king's power and sacredness.

Xerxes approved of Haman's idea. So he said to him, **"Go at once.... Get the robe and the horse and do just as you have suggested** (Haman must have had a huge smile on his face up to this point) **for Mordecai the Jew, who sits at the king's gate. Do not neglect anything you have recommended"** (v. 10). Haman was sent out to proclaim his antagonist as the man whom the king delighted to honor. Imagine the humiliation. Haman's only consolation would have been the thought of killing Mordecai and the Jews.

> ### WORDS FROM WESLEY
> *Esther 6:10*
>
> How mean the gifts which earthly kings
> On favourites bestow,
> What childish toys the noblest things
> And most esteem'd below!
> But whom the King of kings delights
> To honour as His son,
> He to an heavenly feast invites,
> And places on His throne. (PW, vol. 9, 229)

After honoring Mordecai throughout the streets of Susa most of the day, Haman returned home for some comfort. What he found was more bad news, because his friends and wife told him, "'Since Mordecai, before whom your downfall has started, is of Jewish origin, you cannot stand against him—you will surely come to ruin!' While they were talking with him, the king's eunuchs arrived and hurried Haman away to the banquet Esther had prepared" (6:13–14).

Esther's Second Dinner and Final Request (Est. 7:1–10)

So the king and Haman went to dine with Queen Esther (v. 1). Xerxes was probably looking forward to this meal; Haman probably did not have much of an appetite. **As they were drinking wine on that second day, the king again asked, "Queen Esther, what is your petition? It will be given you. What is your request? Even up to half the kingdom, it will be granted"** (v. 2). This is the third time the king has asked (5:3, 6), and Xerxes is ready to hear Esther's plea.

Then Queen Esther answered, "If I have found favor with you, O king, and if it pleases your majesty, grant me my life—this is my petition. And spare my people—this is my request. For I and my people have been sold (referring to Haman's bribe in 3:9) **for destruction and slaughter and annihilation"** (7:3–4). The use of these three words together is a matter of intensity and a powerful expression. **"If we had merely been sold as male and female slaves, I would have kept quiet, because no such distress would justify disturbing the king"** (v. 4). Esther may have thought that as long as her people lived, there would be hope. Or she might have been weighing her words carefully in order to influence the king to take the situation seriously.

WORDS FROM WESLEY
Esther 7:3

My life—It is my only request, that thou wouldst not give me up to the malice of that man who designs to take away my life. Even a stranger, a criminal, shall be permitted to petition for his life. But that a friend, a wife, a queen, should have occasion to make such a petition, was very affecting. (ENOT)

King Xerxes asked Queen Esther, "Who is he? Where is the man who has dared to do such a thing?" (v. 5). The king's anger flared up once again. The first time we saw it was when Vashti refused his request in chapter 1. However, this time it is justified. Someone had plotted to kill his queen and all her people, and the king was coming to her defense.

Esther said, "The adversary and enemy is this vile Haman." Then Haman was terrified before the king and queen (v. 6). This is the only rational response for one caught in his own trap. Haman realized his life was about to end because **the king had already decided his fate** (v. 7). But before Haman could utter a word in his own defense, **the king got up in a rage, left his wine and went out into the palace garden** (v. 7). Why the king left is uncertain. Maybe he was attempting to gather his thoughts before pronouncing his judgment. Whatever the reason, Xerxes stepped outside for a moment, **but Haman . . . stayed behind to beg Queen Esther for his life** (v. 7). She was his only hope, and he knew it.

WORDS FROM WESLEY
Esther 7:6

Afraid—And it was time for him to fear, when the queen was his prosecutor, the king his judge, his own conscience a witness against him. And the surprising turns of providence that very morning, could not but increase his fear. (ENOT)

However, proud Haman was a clumsy beggar, because **just as the king returned from the palace garden to the banquet hall, Haman was falling on the couch where Esther was reclining** (v. 8). The Persians reclined at couches to eat, so Haman approached the queen to implore her for mercy.

The king exclaimed, "Will he even molest the queen while she is with me in the house?" (v. 8). Whether the king really thought Haman was attempting to rape the queen is immaterial. The automatic result of simply charging him with such a crime called for Haman's immediate execution.

So **as soon as the word left the king's mouth**, the servants and guards arrested him and **covered Haman's face. Then Harbona, one of the eunuchs attending the king, said, "A gallows seventy-five feet high stands by Haman's house. He had it made for Mordecai, who spoke up to help the king"** (vv. 8–9).

When he heard that Haman had planned to kill the man who had saved his life, **the king said, "Hang him on it!"** So they hanged Haman on the gallows he had prepared for Mordecai. Then the king's fury subsided (vv. 9–10).

The king gave Haman's estate to Esther (8:1) and promoted her cousin and guardian to Haman's position in the kingdom. Xerxes also gave Mordecai his signet ring that the king had retrieved from Haman (vv. 1–2). Esther asked the king to repeal the decree against the Jews, but he could not because "no document written in the king's name and sealed with his ring can be revoked" (v. 8). However, the king suggested that Queen Esther and Mordecai write a second decree that would allow the Jews to defend themselves against their enemies (vv. 8–11). On the date chosen by the pur or lot (3:7), "the Jews struck down all their enemies with the sword, killing and destroying them" (9:5). After the victory over those who hated them, the Jewish people feasted and celebrated. Mordecai sent out a decree that this feast should be repeated annually (vv. 29–32). This established the Feast of Purim that continues to be celebrated by the Jews to this day.

The Epilogue (Est. 10:3)

Esther comes to a close with this statement: **Mordecai the Jew was second in rank to King Xerxes, preeminent among the Jews, and held in high esteem by his many fellow Jews, because he worked for the good of his people and spoke up for the welfare of all the Jews** (v. 3). Mordecai was a benevolent and charitable government official who was interested in helping others, particularly the Jews. The events of this book were orchestrated by the Lord to keep His covenant with His chosen people. By saving the Jews from annihilation, God was able to "bless all peoples on earth" through Jesus Christ (Gen. 12:1–3).

DISCUSSION

See how God intervened in history to turn the tables on Haman. Watch for evidence that God's rule is greater than that of any earthly king.

1. How has this Old Testament book shown God's hand in the lives of His people?
2. How did God use Xerxes's sleepless night to awaken him to the honor he owed Mordecai?
3. What had Haman wrongly concluded?
4. How do you think Haman felt when the king ordered him to honor Mordecai?
5. What do you think of the saying, "What goes around comes around"? Would you apply the saying to Haman? Why or why not?
6. How did Xerxes counteract his decree against the Jews?
7. What is the significance of the Feast of Purim?
8. How has God turned the tables on someone who opposed you because of your faith?

PRAYER

Father, thank You that You will never forsake us in our troubles. Help us see that You are always at work on our behalf.

WORDS FROM WESLEY WORKS CITED

ENOT: Wesley, J. (1765). *Explanatory Notes upon the Old Testament* (Vol. 1–3). Bristol: William Pine.

PW: *The Poetical Works of John and Charles Wesley.* Edited by D. D. G. Osborn. 13 vols. London: Wesleyan-Methodist Conference Office, 1868.

OTHER BOOKS IN THE
WESLEY BIBLE STUDIES SERIES

Genesis
Exodus
Leviticus through Deuteronomy (available May 2015)
Joshua through Ruth (available May 2015)
1 Samuel through 2 Chronicles
Ezra through Esther
Job through Song of Songs
Isaiah
Jeremiah through Daniel
Hosea through Malachi (available May 2015)
Matthew
Mark
Luke
John
Acts
Romans
1–2 Corinthians
Galatians through Colossians and Philemon
1–2 Thessalonians
1 Timothy through Titus
Hebrews
James
1–2 Peter and Jude
1–3 John
Revelation

Now Available in the Wesley Bible Studies Series

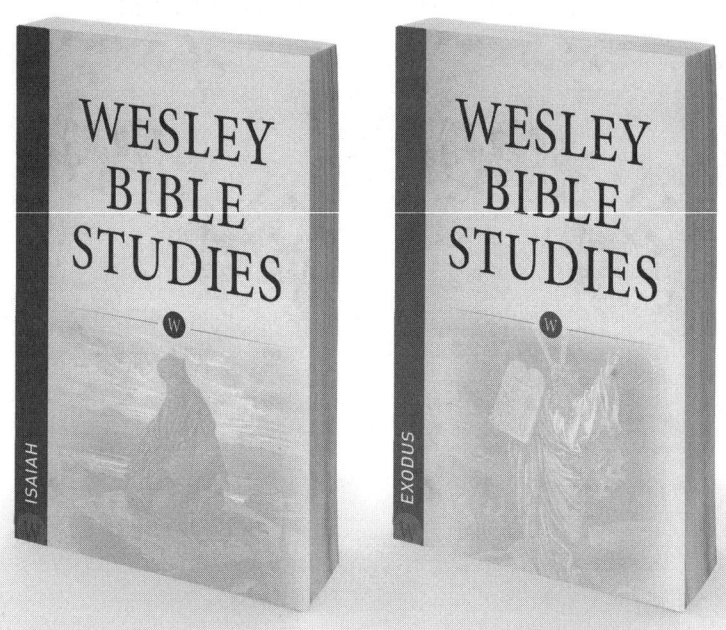

Each book in the Wesley Bible Studies series provides a thoughtful and powerful survey of key Scriptures in one or more biblical books. They combine accessible commentary from contemporary teachers, with relevantly highlighted direct quotes from the complete writings and life experiences of John Wesley, along with the poetry and hymns of his brother Charles. For each study, creative and engaging questions foster deeper fellowship and growth.

Isaiah
978-0-89827-844-6
978-0-89827-845-3 (e-book)

Exodus
978-0-89827-850-7
978-0-89827-851-4 (e-book)

1.800.493.7539   wphstore.com